ALSO BY FRANCO MORETTI

Canon/Archive: Studies in Quantitative Formalism (editor)

The Bourgeois: Between History
and Literature

Distant Reading

The Novel (editor)

Graphs, Maps, Trees: Abstract Models for Literary History

Atlas of the European Novel 1800–1900

Modern Epic: The World-System from Goethe to García Márquez

The Way of the World: The Bildungsroman in European Culture

Signs Taken for Wonders: Essays in the Sociology of Literary Forms

FAR
COUNTRY

FAR COUNTRY

Scenes from American Culture

FRANCO MORETTI

Farrar, Straus and Giroux   New York

Farrar, Straus and Giroux
175 Varick Street, New York 10014

Printed in the United States of America
First edition, 2019

Owing to limitations of space, illustration credits can be found on pages 131–132.

Library of Congress Cataloging-in-Publication Data
Names: Moretti, Franco, 1950– author.
Title: Far country : scenes from American culture / Franco Moretti.
Description: First edition. | New York : Farrar, Straus and Giroux, 2019.
Identifiers: LCCN 2018034448 | ISBN 9780374272708 (hardcover)
Subjects: LCSH: American literature—Study and teaching (Higher)
Classification: LCC PS41.M56 2019 | DDC 810.9/000711—dc23
LC record available at https://lccn.loc.gov/2018034448

Designed by Abby Kagan

Our books may be purchased in bulk for promotional, educational, or
business use. Please contact your local bookseller or the Macmillan Corporate and
Premium Sales Department at 1-800-221-7945, extension 5442, or by e-mail at
MacmillanSpecialMarkets@macmillan.com.

www.fsgbooks.com
www.twitter.com/fsgbooks • www.facebook.com/fsgbooks

1   3   5   7   9   10   8   6   4   2

CONTENTS

FAR
COUNTRY

TEACHING IN AMERICA

I

Stanford, Salerno. Behind this book are two universities: Stanford, where I taught my last course in the spring of 2016; and Salerno, where I taught the first one, in the fall of 1979. In many ways, the two places could not be more different. Stanford is the world's richest private university, in the midst of Silicon Valley; Salerno was a minor public university, located near the *"osso d'Italia"*: the bone that is left once the meat has been eaten away; a barren region, further ravaged by the earthquake of 1980. Many Stanford students come from superb high schools and, if they're interested in English, have at their disposal a department with thirty full-time professors; at Salerno, they came from schools that lacked just about everything, and the entire English department consisted of two inexperienced thirty-year-olds. Due to the vagaries of the heating system, in that winter forty years ago I learned to lecture in my overcoat, to a room filled with overcoats; at

Stanford, anything of this sort would be unimaginable. And so on, and on. But there was one point in common: in both places, students seemed to know very little about literary history. Something had to be done.

Remedial. At Stanford, the English department decided to launch a yearlong course—"Literary History"—which would function as a sort of general introduction to English and American literature, and be taught by a different team in each quarter.* In the discussions that led to that decision, some colleagues described the aim of the course with the word "remedial." Remedial, *remedium*: restoring health after an illness (its root, *mederi*, is the same that "medicine" also comes from); as someone said, let's teach them what they haven't learned in high school. And one understands the logic, of course, but those years in Salerno, where things were definitely worse, had taught me that what matters is not what we ignore, but what we know, and *how* we know it. Students have learned little? Then let's give them more. If they have no idea what poetry is, let's see what happens by compressing into a single lecture the basic concepts of verse and prose, an analysis of "Song of Myself," and some thoughts on lyric and modernity. Too much, in too short a time? Yes; but that's what the university is for: trying to do more than is commonly considered reasonable. Teaching as a wager; the opposite of passing on what one "has" to know about a discipline. Or at least: this is how I (mis)understood the task I

---

* The third section of the course, in which I was involved, was initially taught by me (for the period 1850–1914), Nicholas Jenkins (1914–1945), and Ursula Heise (1945 to the present). Later, the number of instructors was cut to two (myself and Mark McGurl), and eventually one.

had been given, and the spirit in which I taught that class, and have written this book.

II

Hopscotch. With its sixty to seventy students, "Literary History" was large, for a literature class at Stanford. Lectures, just like Salerno. But in the meantime, something had changed. Back then, I had really taught *a course*: a fluid, 200-hour-long reflection on the European *Bildungsroman*, which developed slowly and steadily over two (unforgettable) academic years. At Stanford, I decided right away—but it was more irrational than that: I felt *compelled* right away—to make each ninety-minute lecture stand on its own. The absence of continuity was declared, and almost flaunted: between the first class, on "Poetic Form and the Experience of Modernity," and the return of the same topic a month later, there were two classes on "The Modern Literary Field," two on "Style and Socialization," one on "Radical Modernism," and one on "The Modern Metropolis and the Form of the Novel." Six meetings separated the first two classes on the literary field from the third one; seven, the first lecture on the novel and metropolitan experience from the second one. This hopscotch disposition was perfect for the two aspects of literary history I wanted to highlight: on the one hand, recognizing the permanence of a few major questions from generation to generation (What kind of plot allows us to "see" the structure of a modern city? Is tragedy still possible, in the capitalist world?); on the other, realizing how varied were the answers that had been found in the course of time. Janus-like, each lecture oscillated between the stability of literary history and the earthquakes that from time to time redesigned its landscape.* This was not the kind of literary history—one author after another, in a long uninterrupted chain—that I had been taught in my university years: where continuity was so pervasive and "natural" it seemed to make explanations superfluous. The irregular chessboard I put in front of my students was too strange to be taken for granted. Literary history had become a problem, that asked for a solution.

Form against form. "Whitman and Free Verse," read the title of the first class on poetry and modernity; given that the lecture's main point was the bifurcation between two incompatible conceptions of modern poetry, "Walt Whitman or Charles Baudelaire?" would have been much better. And so it went, class after class; every topic would split into two, and generate an opposition. The pleasure of early mass culture could take the form of a cheap anonymous dime novel, or of a Sherlock Holmes story in *The Strand*; the pleasure of 1950s adventures, the spacious sunlight of a Western, or the ill-lit claustrophobia of a film noir. At times, the opposition ran across two successive lectures (free indirect style/stream of consciousness; Gertrude Stein/Virginia Woolf; *Endgame/Death of a Salesman*); in the final class, on the Dutch golden age and twentieth-century American painting, it

---

*Many disparate influences had contributed to this view of history: Russian formalism and 1960s structuralism were the initial—and strictly literary—sources of inspiration; later, my wanderings through the natural sciences made me encounter Gould's and Eldredge's "punctuated equilibria" and Kuhn's "paradigm shifts"; while in the last few years, Brecht's notion of the "epic theater"—where "each scene exists for itself," the story advances by "leaps," and the meaning of the whole can only be grasped through the "montage" of disparate elements—has become very important for the way I think about these matters.

even spanned centuries. In every case, conflict emerged as the key mechanism behind the history I was trying to teach; conflict between "high literature" and pulp fiction, of course, but just as much between texts that belonged to the same niche of the literary field, such as James's "Beast in the Jungle" and Joyce's "The Dead." Antagonism ruled, everywhere; and it did so through the medium of form. For Whitman, the poetry of modernity required a maximum of simplicity; for Baudelaire, of complexity. Form against form. "Dashing Diamond Dick" tried to conquer a broad audience by being explicit and excessive; "The Adventure of the Speckled Band," by being ambiguous and restrained. Form against form. To understand the logic behind this conflict, each lecture explored three interconnected aspects of literary form: its use of language and rhetoric; the historical context of its emergence; and its potential appeal for contemporary audiences. Technique, history, and pleasure: the "how," "why," and "what for" of literature. It didn't matter where the argument started from: the discussion of free indirect style took off from a few sentences in Austen, and that on the stream of consciousness, which followed two days later, from Simmel's sociology of metropolitan life; the lecture on Vermeer began with a narrative analysis of his domestic scenes, and that on Rembrandt with the texture of the skin of his self-portraits. It didn't matter where one started, as long as all aspects of form were activated, doing justice to the concept's complexity. Complexity, though not perfection: committed to disparate imperatives, and caught in the never-ending campaigns of the literary field, great forms are necessarily contingent, tentative—"problematic," to use a keyword of the early Lukács. That, despite being engaged on so many fronts, they accomplish as much as they do—this, not perfection, is their greatness.

Petite phrase. "Every form," reads a memorable passage of *Theory of the Novel*, "is the resolution of a fundamental dissonance of existence."* As World War I reduced millions of men to a state of terrified impotence, Hemingway's prose style provided an answer (if not exactly a "resolution") to the trauma they had undergone. Here, the technical side of form—Hemingway's spectacular use of prepositional phrases, for instance—emerges as the key mediation between the historical world and readerly pleasure. And if "prepositional phrases" sounds a bit esoteric . . . it is, and it's deliberate. Because this is how form works: with devices that are often microscopic, and hard to recognize. (Which is also, incidentally, *why* it works: by remaining undetected, microscopic devices don't disturb the immediacy of our pleasure.) But not everyone approves of this way of connecting (an aspect of) form and (an aspect of) historical experience; when Walter Benjamin sent his essay "The Paris of the Second Empire in Baudelaire" to the journal of the Institut für Sozialforschung, Adorno rejected it because of the "crass and rough" connection instituted in the essay between "the Baudelairian world of forms" and "the necessities of life":

---

*György Lukács, *Theory of the Novel*, 1914–15, MIT Press, 1974, p. 62. On this point, Lukács is not alone; Kenneth Burke famously defined art forms as "'strategies' for living" (*Attitudes Toward History*, 1937, 3rd ed., UC Press, 1984, p. 43), while George Kubler wrote that "every important work of art can be regarded [. . .] as a hard won solution to some problem" (*The Shape of Time: Remarks on the History of Things*, 1972, Yale UP, 2008, p. 30). Building on Lévi-Strauss's *Structural Anthropology*, Fredric Jameson defined narrative as "the imaginary resolution of a real contradiction" (*The Political Unconscious*, Cornell UP, 1981, p. 77), while for Michael Baxandall "the historical explanation of pictures" consists in "reconstructing both the specific problem [they were] designed to solve and the specific circumstances out of which [they were] addressing it" (*Patterns of Intention: On the Historical Explanation of Pictures*, Yale UP, 1985, pp. 14–15).

I regard it as methodologically unfortunate to give conspicuous individual features from the realm of the superstructure a "materialistic" turn by relating them immediately and perhaps even causally to corresponding features of the infrastructure. Materialist determination of cultural traits is only possible if it is mediated through the *total social process*.*

In the absence of such totalizing mediation, concluded Adorno, work such as Benjamin's would find itself "at the crossroads of magic and positivism. This spot is bewitched . . ." A superb formulation: but wrong. Contingent as forms are, some of their elements may easily achieve a certain autonomy, and analyzing them in (near-)isolation is perfectly legitimate; besides, what captures our attention and fixes itself in our memory is seldom a work's entire structure; more often, it's something on a much smaller scale, like Vinteuil's *"petite phrase"* for Swann, or Vermeer's *"petit pain du mur jaune"* for Bergotte (and notice those two *"petit/e,"* with which Proust unobtrusively implies how *little* is needed to trigger our emotional response). Whence a recurring aspect of "Literary History," and now of this book: isolating "conspicuous individual features" (a metaphor, an episode, a grammatical structure) from the work under discussion; analyzing how they work; and then trying to imagine how they had reacted—"immediately and perhaps even causally"—to a specific historical "dissonance." If this reconstruction felt convincing, the "total social process" could wait.

Diagram of forces. *Far Country*, reads the title of this book: far in space, obviously enough, for someone who grew up in Europe

*Theodor W. Adorno, letter of November 10, 1938, in Adorno et al., *Aesthetics and Politics*, Verso, London, 1977, p. 129.

and has now returned to live there. But just as distant in time: Weber, Simmel, the early Lukács, Russian Formalism, Benjamin,
Spitzer, Adorno: these pages could (almost) have been written a
hundred years ago. One reason was certainly my growing intol-
erance for the "presentism" (a dismal word, but appropriate to its
object) of the American academy, which inevitably undermines all
sense of the past. But the deeper reason had to do, once again, with
the concept of form: more precisely, with the "anti-chaotic function"
Aby Warburg had associated with it in the Introduction to *The
Atlas Mnemosyne*.* Faced with the incessant turmoil of the empiri-
cal world, artistic form operates a selection of the materials to
be represented, and fixes them into a structure; and it does
so through an *agonistic* process: *anti*-chaotic: "an objectivizing
conflict [. . .] between a forming power and a material to be overcome," as Panofsky put it in his essay on the "will-to-art."† It's the
Realpolitik of form: the gray zone where beauty comes into contact with power, and even with violence. "We both like working
with hard materials," says Ibsen's last hero, the sculptor Rubek,
to, of all people, a bear hunter: "and both of us force our material down under control at last. Become lord and master over it.
We never give up till we've overcome it, no matter how much
it fights back."‡ Force, control, master. From the opposite end of
the cultural spectrum, here is D'Arcy Wentworth Thompson,
formulating the project of his morphological masterpiece, *On
Growth and Form*:

---

*Aby Warburg, *Der Bilderatlas Mnemosyne. Einleitung*, 1929, in *Gesammelte
Schriften*, II.1, Martin Warnke, ed., De Gruyter, Berlin, 2000, p. 3.
†Erwin Panofsky, "Der Begriff des Kunstwollens," *Zeitschrift für Ästhetik und
allgemeine Kunstwissenschaft* XIV (1920), p. 339.
‡Henrik Ibsen, *When We Dead Awaken*, 1899, in *The Complete Major Prose Plays*,
translated and introduced by Rolf Fjelde, New York, 1978, p. 1044.

The form of any portion of matter [. . .] may in all cases alike be described as due to the action of force. In short, the form of an object is a "diagram of forces," in this sense, at least, that from it we can judge of, or deduce the forces that are acting or have acted upon it.*

Deduce forces from forms: it could be the motto of the great Wilhelmine sociologists. Whether reflecting on aesthetic phenomena, administrative systems, conceptual structures, or the norms of individual conduct, the concrete power of abstract patterns—the *force* of *forms*—was a constant theme in the work of Weber, Simmel, and Sombart. Nor is it a coincidence that these were the great theorists of modern capitalism and bourgeois existence: the specificity of Germany's late industrialization, with the dominant role played by banks, the state, and scientific research, revealed to this generation of thinkers how thoroughly could social existence be shaped by external forces. Form was power in the act of imposing a stable order onto modern societies. Form as force, then—but also *force as form*: as a capacity to shape and organize, and not only coerce. It is the awareness of this double perspective that we need, today just as much as a century ago.

Autonomous factor. As these initial pages have made clear, in this book "form" mostly means: style. Extracting short passages from a work, and analyzing their language, worked well in class, and it became a "practice" before I realized it was happening. (Later, I made it explicit with two lectures on "Style and Socialization.") Style—and in fact styles, plural, because each age generates a whole spectrum of them—allowed me to compare

* *On Growth and Form*, 1917, rev. ed., 1942, Dover, New York, 1992, p. 16.

texts with each other (they all used nouns, verb tenses, tropes, sentences of varying length and complexity), thus sharpening the sense of how varied literature can be. "As long as we know only a single style," Simmel once observed, we inevitably perceive it "as being identical with its contents"; it's only when we become familiar with *many* styles that we can see each of them "as an autonomous factor."* What he meant was something like this: there were many ways of representing colonialism, in late nineteenth-century Europe: Kipling's melancholy and whimsical sense of duty was one of them, as was Haggard's adventurous brutality, Verne's para-scientific curiosity, or Salgari's melodrama—plus, of course, all kinds of nonliterary discourses. Each of these styles was "an autonomous factor" in the sense that it did not concide "with its contents," and in fact—to merge Simmel's and Panofsky's formulations into a synthetic statement—was bent on "overcoming" such contents with its own specific "shaping power." Peculiar to, say, Conrad's style in *Heart of Darkness* was the way in which aesthetic elegance—Marlow's web of similes, litotes, polyphony, digressions, irony . . . —could cautiously come to terms with pure and simple ferocity. Form and force, again: where, by reverse-engineering "technicalities" such as Marlow's digressions, the analysis of style can open a window into a past—into an *ideology* from the past—that would have otherwise remained forever closed.†

---

*Georg Simmel, *The Philosophy of Money*, rev. ed. [1907], Routledge, London and New York, 1990, p. 462.

†By reverse-engineering I mean the following three steps: first, extracting a specific technique from a given text, and seeing it as a "formal resolution" in Lukács's sense; second, conjecturing what was the historical "dissonance" the technique was designed to resolve; and, third, trying to imagine what kind of pleasure—or, in some cases, which way of avoiding pain and

Belle époque. Beginning with the opening lecture, on the first in-
stallment of *Our Mutual Friend*, most of "Literary History" dealt
with narrative texts of one kind or another; so, something felt
vaguely wrong in the complete predominance of stylistics over the
analysis of narrative structures. In part, this reflected the weak-
ness of contemporary narratology *vis-à-vis* the results of linguis-
tic analysis; in part, it was a consequence of the disparate genres I
had chosen for the course (novels, novellas, short stories, films,
plays . . .), and of the difficulty of finding a common denominator
among them. But the main reason had to do with literature itself:
with the fact that, in the last two centuries, the balance between
story and style had slowly but steadily tilted towards the latter. A
week after *Our Mutual Friend*, where the two aspects had still the
same weight, the structure of *Heart of Darkness*—where the plot
of Kurtz's exploitation of the Congo, though obviously important,
was thoroughly "overcome" by Marlow's ironic mediation—had
already indicated the direction of the process; one more week
("The Beast in the Jungle" and "The Dead"), and the primacy of
"meaning" over narrative had become even starker. With Modernism it became extreme, and not only in those obvious cases like
Ulysses and *Endgame* in which "nothing happened," and focusing
on style rather than plot seemed virtually inevitable. Even where
a strong plot *was* present, writers seemed to do all they could to
counter its force: the destinies of the heroines of *Three Lives* would
have an even greater impact if they were not concealed behind the
impassable façade of Stein's repetitions; the calamities of *To the
Lighthouse* would remain more memorable if they weren't "struck
into stability"—stability: the opposite of narrative—by the painting

---

discomfort—could be provided by such resolution. Once again: the "how,"
"why," and "what for" of aesthetic form.

that concludes the novel. The exceptions confirmed the rule: only in fiction produced with a large market in mind—dime novels, detective fiction, Westerns, film noirs—did plot continue to matter; in the "autonomous" space of high literature, it was style that ruled. In some cases (James, Conrad, Woolf), a *class* element was also unmistakably present, as stylistic subtlety duplicated the "refinement"—tact, ease, reserve, taste, elegance—with which *fin de siècle* elites tried to endow bourgeois existence with an aristocratic patina: the last, vain attempt at forging a modern European ruling class.

III

A literature for America. Instead of exploring *fin-de-siècle* Europe, the structure of "Literary History" turned my attention towards American culture. First came the lectures on film; years earlier, while working on the worldwide diffusion of nineteenth-century European novels, I had often thought about twentieth-century Hollywood, and the lectures on the Western and film noir followed naturally from those reflections. The idea that the social function of literature had migrated outside literature suggested other attempts of a similar direction (TV series, ads, graphic novels, songs); in the end, all I managed to do was a double comparison (Vermeer/Hopper and Rembrandt/Warhol) that allowed me to cast a retrospective glance at the long arc of bourgeois self-presentation. Meanwhile, the course's overall design had prompted the lectures on Hemingway and Miller, to complement others on analogous topics; add to these the class on Whitman, which had been there from the start, and the result was the odd quintet that composes this book. Odd, but with something important in common. First of all, a marked discontinuity with the great generation of turn-of-the-century *emigrés*; James, Stein, Pound, Eliot had all written for a small and cosmopolitan audience; the authors discussed in this book had instead clearly in mind an *American* public—and, in principle at least, a rather broad one. Biography blended with geography: the previous group had settled in England, France, Italy; aside from Hemingway, the others never really left the United States, and the subject matter of their work was itself profoundly American: Whitman, Hopper, Miller, the Western, of course, and in fact even Warhol, who owed his international fame to two images—Campbell's soup cans and Marilyn Monroe—that were as American as Ford's Monument Valley. This literature for America was, however, also—and, in fact, increasingly—a literature *from* America, that traveled all over the world and presented itself as an alternative to European forms. Whence the recurrent comparison of American and European authors in the chapters that follow: Whitman and Baudelaire, Hemingway and Joyce, the Western and film noir, Miller and Brecht . . . Form against form, again; where the stakes, this time, were the foundations of American cultural hegemony. Powerful and elusive notion, hegemony: where works that are produced in a specific culture (*American* hegemony) are then accepted and absorbed in very different contexts (American *hegemony*). Function becomes partly autonomous from genesis, and the ratio of the two sides of the formula—the "American" and the "hegemonic"—fluctuates from case to case. In the chapters on Hemingway and the Western, I try to understand how American forms made sense *vis-à-vis* the ferocity of twentieth-century European history; with Warhol, it's the commodity that moves to the foreground; while Whitman returns throughout the book as the fundamental model for a democratic aesthetics.* These are, clearly enough, just a handful of disparate instances, which specialists may find questionable; but I decided to go ahead just the same, because the decoding of cultural hegemony—which in our times, for the first time in history, has reached a truly planetary dimension—can only succeed as a collective effort, involving scholars from many different fields. Let's hope that, despite its shortcomings, this study may be a step in the right direction.

IV

Clarity. A discontinuous history in which microscopic devices battled each other across the oceans in ever-shifting historical configurations; and all this, twice a week, in ninety-minute monologues delivered with a heavy Italian accent. Only one thing could make it bearable: clarity. For me, this has long been a fundamental value, and a *political* one; something I had learned not from literary theory (not at all . . .), but from a group of Italian intellectuals—Lucio Colletti, Rossana Rossanda, Umberto Eco, Beniamino Placido—who were all engaged, in one way or another, with the new left politics and Marxist thought of the 1960s and '70s.† Their public styles couldn't have been more different—

---

*In the case of Hopper and Miller, the hegemonic theme is *de facto* absent, as theirs is an America in the grip of economic depression (Hopper), or without any hope of future progress (Miller). The relevance of these two authors to other aspects of my argument, and the light they shed on American life, explains, I hope, their inclusion here.

†Colletti, a philosopher, combined rigorous Marxian philology and a ferocious hostility to dialectics; Rossanda, one of the founders of *Il Manifesto*,

Colletti's conceptual haughtiness as remote from Placido's serio-comic wisdom as Rossanda's purposeful conviction was from Eco's desecrating irony—yet they all converged towards what can only be called *the democratization of culture*. Democratization: breaking complex issues down into their elements, without taking anything for granted. Democratization *of culture*: preserving all the key steps in the argument, and asking readers to *work*, and not just to follow. Each sentence should be perfectly clear; each paragraph, demanding and complex. Clarity is not a way of avoiding what is difficult, it's a way of *understanding* it; usually, via a step-by-step process of analysis that dispels "the illusion works of art generate, of being an absolutely integrated being," and reveals them as "having-been-constructed" instead.* Desacralization: masterpieces are not miracles, they are *work*: many disparate elements, intricately put together. Analysis pries open the mechanism, and clarity makes the results accessible to all; which is why "gaining *clarity*" could be presented in "Science as a Vocation" as the fundamental aim of teaching, and of intellectual activity in general. Where I would go beyond Weber is in viewing clarity not merely as an instrumental value—"*if* you take such and such a stand, then [. . .] you must take such and such a *means*"†—but as an end in itself. Clarity is the principle of equality in the world of ideas; and the principle of intransigence, too; it makes arguments

---

wrote memorable articles on the *putsch* against Allende and the Portuguese revolution; Eco, not yet a novelist, used his semiotic intelligence for all-round cultural polemics; and Placido, a freelance intellectual, was to become the leading cultural journalist for *La Repubblica*.

*Theodor W. Adorno, *Alban Berg: Master of the Smallest Link*, 1968, Cambridge UP, 1991, pp. 35–37.

†Max Weber, "Science as a Vocation," in H. H. Gerth and C. Wright Mills, eds., *From Max Weber: Essays in Sociology*, Oxford UP, 1958, p. 151.

sharper, more one-sided; free from fear, and from all forms of hypocrisy. The mild yet inflexible words of one of the founders of modern science remain a model in this respect: "I love to speak of persons with civility, though of things with freedom."* Speaking with freedom: this is what clarity is ultimately about.

Paragraphs. So much work, lecturing. You study, take notes, reflect, plan, prepare, rehearse, speak . . . A few people listen, and then it's gone; smoke in the wind. Something is wrong, in all this: either introductory classes in the humanities are not very important (and then they shouldn't be taught), or they have something significant to say (and then they shouldn't be confined to a purely propaedeutic function). Whence this book: which takes five university lectures for first- or second-year students—five easy pieces—and brings them out of the classroom, making them "public"; addressing readers who are definitely interested in literature (or they wouldn't still be reading), but not at all in a professional sense. Speaking *from* a university classroom, then, though not (only) *to* it: this is the idea. But let me be clear: I have no intention of "hiding" the origin of these chapters in the act of teaching; if anything, I may have erred in the opposite direction, in trying to remain as close as I could to their original form.† Close, though not identi-

---

*Robert Boyle, "A Proemial Essay, wherein, with some Considerations touching Experimental Essays in general, Is interwoven such an Introduction to all those written by the Author, as is necessary to be perused for the better understanding of them," in *The Works of the Honourable Robert Boyle*, ed. Thomas Birch, 2nd ed., J.&F. Rivington, London, 1772, vol. I, p. 312.
†Nor to their form only. Once I finished writing, I became aware that the thesis of the book was not as explicit as it could have been: that, for instance, the constellation of values that characterize American hegemony—democracy, violence, and consumer capitalism—had emerged only sporadically, and had not been taken as far as it could have. At first I thought of simply

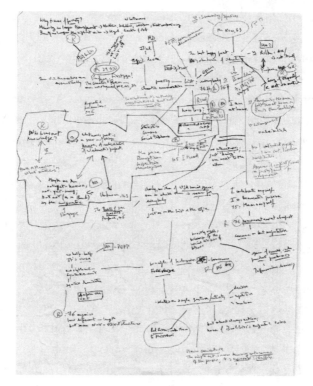

Figure 1.

cal; which wouldn't have been possible in any case, as the lectures
were not written, and all I had to orient myself was a page like the
plan for the Whitman/Baudelaire lecture in Figure 1: a private
palimpsest, not always easy to read, which left the sequence and
weight of the various points largely undefined. These were

correcting this state of affairs; then I realized that, if the problem was there in
the first place, it was because my idea of a university course is that of a series
of meetings with (hopefully) some interesting things to say, but where the
lecturer's convictions remain more in the background than is usually the case
in a book. Right or wrong, it seemed important that the book should preserve
this aspect of the original course.

"modular" lecture plans, made of a dozen conceptual blocks, each of which could become twice as long, or disappear altogether, according to the inspiration (let's call it that) of the day. Knowing that the lecture was not quite "done" helped me reach the right tension before class; for teaching, it worked well. At my desk, not so much. In writing, I have occasionally altered the order of the segments (which was open in any case), while using footnotes and parentheses to reproduce those small digressions—at times, just a sentence and a wave of the hand—that are typical of an oral argument. Rather than adopting a "spoken" tone, though, I have tried to fashion a written form—the staccato paragraphs you have been reading all along—that seems to me to be loosely comparable to the "points" of a long lecture class. You take a deep breath, start speaking, and five minutes later find yourself in a very different place; at times, it's not clear how you got there, and what to do next; but it's a lecture, you must go on, so you drink a sip of water, look around for a moment, and start speaking again. Trying to capture this rhythm in the written register has resulted in this odd little book: short in pages, and compressed in style. The university, in the form of an essay.

Wonder and critique. But why should readers be interested in what is being taught to a roomful of twenty-year-olds who are not even sure they want to study literature in earnest? Actually, that is precisely the reason: in an introductory course you have to say what is most important about a given discipline; in this case, convince those in front of you *that literature is worth studying, and not just enjoying*. Fantastic challenge, for those who have spent their entire adult lives studying and teaching literature, and who no longer perceive how strange that is. Whereas, let's be honest, there is something slightly perverse in turning pleasure into work; and there is much to be said for a situation in which you find yourself having to prove all that you usually take for granted: not only that reading the thousand pages of *Our Mutual Friend* is a good idea, but that it gets even better if you reflect on Dickens's use of the neuter pronoun, and periodically consult Charles Booth's block-by-block map of Victorian London. The example is not an imaginary one: "Literary History" was a course with two very different sides: half literary theory, half social science of one kind or another. Literature was viewed *from within and from without*, in a regular oscillation that gave the class its peculiar flavor: we are reading a novella, so you have to know Harald Weinrich's thesis on the role of the "unheard-of" in this narrative form; we are reading a novella about colonialism, so here is Joseph Chamberlain's speech at the Royal Colonial Institute, and a map of anti-colonial uprisings. The pendular movement reminded me of the title of my first book: *Signs Taken for Wonders*. Back then, in 1983, the idea had been that literary works were too easily "taken for wonders," and one had to bring them back down to earth, showing them to be prosaic sociocultural "signs" instead. These days, when aesthetic admiration is more often a retrograde personality cult— *Shakespeare: The Invention of the Human*; *How Proust Can Change Your Life*—than a genuine intellectual experience, the first task consisted in reawakening the students' capacity for wonder. I wanted them to be as struck by Whitman's meandering verses, a panoramic shot of *Red River*, or Miller's "Attention must be paid" as their grandparents might have been. And at that point—once wonder had been restored to its pedestal, as passionately and naively as possible—at that point, with a sudden about-face, we would all "stand outside and study," to quote Brecht on the epic

theater.* Having (hopefully) re-enchanted the experience of literature, the lecture would subject it to that "estrangement" (Brecht
again) "that is necessary to all understanding";† and that, usually,
consists in bringing to light literature's collusion with social
power. There are scholars for whom only the love for literature matters; others, who only approve of the unmasking. More
ambivalently, I care about both: radical critique is necessary *precisely because of the magic of which literature is capable*. Enjoy all
the magic, and then filter it through the skepticism of critique:
this, for me, is aesthetic education.

Shopping for classes. But is it? Let me return to the Salerno of
forty years ago: to those students, so many of whom came from
families with very low levels of formal education. For them, being at the university was a promise of dramatic social mobility. But
not only a promise; taking a university course was *itself* a sign of
mobility; an intellectual experience that used to be beyond their
reach, and wasn't anymore. Besides being a means to some other
end, the university was something to be enjoyed immediately and
for its own sake; *an end in itself*; a luxury that, like so many other
luxuries before it, had turned into a widely accepted right, like
washing one's body with clean water in Brecht's *Life of Galileo* (an
act not unrelated to good thinking, in his opinion).‡ "It is possible

---

* "Notes on the Opera *Rise and Fall of the City of Mahagonny*," 1931, in John
Willett, ed., *Brecht on Theatre: The Development of an Aesthetic*, Farrar, Straus
and Giroux, New York, 1992, p. 37.
† "Theatre for Pleasure or Theatre for Instruction," ca. 1936, in John Willett,
ed., *Brecht on Theatre*, cit., p. 71.
‡ "Isn't the pleasure of drinking milk and washing oneself one and the same
thing with the pleasure which he takes in new ideas?" wonders Brecht about
his character in the *Kleines Organon*: "Don't forget: he thinks for the pleasure

to live and not know," Richard Feynman has written, in a book tellingly entitled *The Pleasure of Finding Things Out;*[*] but knowing makes life so much richer. It was the emotion of knowledge for knowledge's sake—"he thinks for the pleasure of thinking!"—that kept us all warm during those chilly Salerno afternoons. Today, it's cold again: university life, ruled by the grim Victorian slogan that has found its second home in Silicon Valley: *useful* knowledge. "The American boy's conception of the teacher who faces him," wrote Weber in "Science as a Vocation," is that "he sells me his knowledge and his methods for my father's money, just as the greengrocer sells my mother cabbage. And that is all."[†] A century ago, he might have been a little unfair to the American boy; in the decades that followed, universities seemed determined to prove him right. At the beginning of each term, American students "shop for classes": they show up in this and that course, to figure out whether they like the topic, or the instructor, or whatever. In itself, of course, this isn't at all wrong. What *is* wrong, is a culture that describes it as shopping. "In a complex world there are many kinds of action," wrote Kenneth Burke in *Attitudes Toward History*:

> in naming them, we form our characters, since the names embody attitudes [and] shape our relations with our fellows [. . .] Call a man a villain, and you have the choice of either attacking or cringing. Call him mistaken, and you invite yourself to attempt setting him right.[‡]

---

of thinking!" "A Short Organum for the Theater," 1948, in John Willett, ed., *Brecht on Theatre*, cit., p. 198.

[*] Richard P. Feynman, *The Pleasure of Finding Things Out*, Perseus, Cambridge, MA, 1999, p. 112.

[†] Max Weber, "Science as a Vocation," cit., p. 149.

[‡] Kenneth Burke, *Attitudes Toward History*, 1937, 3rd ed., UC Press, 1984, p. 4.

A group of twenty-year-olds enter a classroom, sit down, and listen; call what brought them there "exploration," and you are dealing with curiosity, surprise, unpredictability; confusion, perhaps, but open to the world around them. Call it "shopping," and you are dealing with customers bent on getting a "deal"; they already know what they want and they want it *now*, without surprises or complications. Names do indeed shape our relations with the world; they outline what is considered valuable, thus making it more likely to happen. In this metamorphosis of students into customers—and in the myriad associated mutations, all going in the same direction—the university has fulfilled its financial dreams, and betrayed its intellectual purpose. And this, for the moment, is where we are.

II

WALT WHITMAN OR CHARLES BAUDELAIRE?

I

Disenchantment. 1801. Friedrich Hölderlin, "Bread and Wine":

> But, my friend! we come too late. The Gods are living, yes,
>> But up above our heads, in another world.
> Endlessly they act there, and seem to care little
>> Whether we live or not . . .*

Too late. Time was, bread and wine meant—and in fact *were*—the body and blood of Christ. Now, meanings have become opaque. In "a world that has been abandoned by god [. . .] the immanence of meaning in life becomes problematic," wrote Lukács a

---

* "Aber Freund! wir kommen zu spät. Zwar leben die Götter, / Aber über dem Haupt droben in anderer Welt. / Endlos wirken sie da und scheinen's wenig zu achten, / Ob wir leben . . ."

century later, in *Theory of the Novel*.* "The fate of our times is characterized by rationalization and intellectualization and, above all, by the 'disenchantment of the world,'" added Weber in the same years, giving currency to a key metaphor of Western modernity.† Disenchantment: "One can, in principle, master all things by calculation," thus liberating the world from all "mysterious incalculable forces" [139]; but something is missing from this view of reality: "Who [. . .] still believes that the findings of astronomy, biology, physics or chemistry could teach us anything about the *meaning* of the world?" [142]. A world abandoned by god can be understood much better—but it no longer "speaks" to us:

> . . . meanwhile I often think
> Better to sleep, than to be so without companions,
> Only waiting, and what to do or to say in the meantime
> I do not know, and why poets in the age of misery?‡

Misery, *dürftige Zeit*, not as material, but as spiritual poverty: poverty of meaning. And what can poetry do, in a world deprived of meaning? Has it become—a thing of the past?

Nobody wants poetry now. 1820s. Hölderlin's university friend Hegel is lecturing on aesthetics. Early in the argument comes a passage that is often referred to as "the death of art":

---

* György Lukács, *Theory of the Novel*, cit., pp. 88 and 56.
† Max Weber, "Science as a Vocation," cit., p. 155.
‡ "Indessen dünket mir öfters / Besser zu schlafen, wie so ohne Genossen zu seyn, / So zu harren, und was zu thun indeß und zu sagen, / Weiß ich nicht, und wozu Dichter in dürftiger Zeit?"

Only one [. . .] stage of truth is capable of being represented in the element of art [. . .] Such truth must in virtue of its own specific character be able to go forth into [the sphere of] sense and remain adequate to itself there. This is the case, for example, with the gods of Greece. On the other hand, there is a deeper comprehension of truth which is no longer so akin and friendly to sense [. . .] The Christian view of truth is of this kind, and, above all, the spirit of our world today [has moved] beyond the stage at which art is the supreme mode of our knowledge of the Absolute [. . .] Works of art no longer fill our highest need.*

Art no longer fills our highest needs . . . Nor our lowest ones, either. As Hegel was giving his course in Berlin, a major transformation was taking place in the literary field of the leading European economy. "Despite an increase of 23 percent in the number of titles appearing annually between 1815 and 1828," writes Lee Erickson,

and another 30 percent increase in titles between 1828 and 1832 [. . .], by 1830 almost all [British] publishers refused to publish poetry. John Murray refused any manuscripts of poetry after Byron's death in 1824; Longman said "nobody wants poetry now" and encouraged authors to write cookbooks instead of volumes of verse; John Taylor wrote to John Clare in 1830 saying that his firm "was no longer a publisher of poetry"; and Smith, Elder told Clare in the same year that they would publish poetry only at the author's risk. As Benjamin

* G. W. F. Hegel, *Aesthetics: Lectures on Fine Art*, 1818–30, Clarendon Press, Oxford, 2010, pp. 9–10.

Disraeli said in *Vivian Grey*, "the reign of Poesy is over, at least for half a century."[*]

At least. When *Les Fleurs du Mal* was published, in 1857, Baudelaire "envisaged readers to whom the reading of lyric poetry would present difficulties," wrote Walter Benjamin:

> The introductory poem of the *Fleurs du Mal* is addressed to these readers. Willpower and the ability to concentrate are not their strong points; what they prefer is sensual pleasures [. . .] It is strange to come across a lyric poet who addresses himself to such readers—the least rewarding type of audience.[†]

It is strange; it's the sign of Baudelaire's profound ambivalence towards the literary market: he hates it, and he wants it. Here is the opening of "Au lecteur":

> Stupidity, error, sin, stinginess
> Possess our spirits . . .[‡]

A book of poetry, whose first word is "stupidity." The scene is complete: philosophical history, commercial publishing, and avant-garde poetics—enormously different as they are—have found one thing on which they all agree: nobody wants poetry now.

---

[*] Lee Erickson, *The Economy of Literary Form: English Literature and the Industrialization of Publishing, 1800–1850*, Johns Hopkins UP, 1996, p. 26.
[†] Walter Benjamin, "On Some Motifs in Baudelaire," 1940, in *Selected Writings, IV, 1938–40*, Harvard UP, 2003, p. 313.
[‡] "La sottise, l'erreur, le péché, la lésine, / Occupent nos esprits . . ."

II

Omnivorous lines. Nobody? In the same year as "Au Lecteur," *Leaves of Grass* was also published:

> The Americans of all nations at any time upon the earth have probably the fullest poetical nature. The United States themselves are essentially the greatest poem [. . .] Here is not merely a nation but a teeming nation of nations. Here is action untied from strings necessarily blind to particulars and details magnificently moving in vast masses. Here is the hospitality which forever indicates heroes . . . Here are the roughs and beards and space and ruggedness and nonchalance . . .*

The greatest poem: far from being hostile to poetry, Whitman's United States *are* poetry. Poetry of the here, and of the now: Here is . . . Here is . . . Here is . . . Poetry of superlatives (fullest, greatest, magnificently, forever, heroes, at any time upon the earth), and of plurals (Americans, nations, strings, particulars, details, masses, roughs . . .) Poetry of profusion, for which Whitman has found the perfect form: the "catalogue"; the "divine list," as he calls it in "From pent-up aching rivers": Here is not merely . . . Here is action . . . Here is the hospitality . . . Here are the roughs *and* beards *and* space *and* ruggedness . . . From Homer's catalogue of ships to Milton's *Pandemonium*, the catalogue has been the typical epic device, used to evoke the vastness of a poem's subject. In *Leaves of Grass*, this epic subject is the United States:

> The bugle calls in the ball-room, the gentlemen run for
> their partners, the dancers bow to each other;

*Walt Whitman, *Poetry and Prose*, Library of America, New York, 1982, p. 5.

The youth lies awake in the cedar-roof'd garret, and
    harks to the musical rain;
The Wolverine sets traps on the creek that helps fill the
    Huron;
The squaw, wrapped in her yellow-hemmed cloth, is
    offering moccasins and bead-bags for sale;
The connoisseur peers along the exhibition-gallery with
    half-shut eyes bent sideways;
As the deck-hands make fast the steamboat, the plank is
    thrown for the shore-going passengers . . .
    (**"Song of Myself,"** 15)

Gentlemen, dancers, youth, Wolverine, squaw, connoisseur, deck-hands, passengers . . . Not kings or arch-devils: just a lot of common people (in this section of "Song of Myself," more than eighty of them). The epic, democratized. And then: ball-room, garret, creek, gallery, steamboat, shore . . . Each social type, in its specific habitat. The nineteenth century is creating all sorts of practices designed to "see" the nation in its entirety—census, map, museum, statistics, tableaux, panoramas—and Whitman writes *the poetry of this new national visibility*.* "I know my omnivorous lines, and will not write any less" ("Song of Myself," 43); "unrhymed poetry," adds the "Preface" to *Leaves of Grass* [6], and it's easy to see the link between the two: rhyme drastically reduces what any given line can "ingest," and the nation of nations, which has just unleashed a truly omnivorous territorial expansion—in the twentieth

---

* "Census, Map, Museum" is the title of the chapter of *Imagined Communities* in which Benedict Anderson describes the "grid" of state classifications, and the underlying assumption that the world, like Whitman's America, "was made up of replicable plurals." Benedict Anderson, *Imagined Communities*, Verso, London, 1983, rev. ed., 1991, pp. 184–85.

century, Whitman's times will be the favorite setting for Westerns—chafes at limitations. That's why the catalogue works so well: having no inner constraint, it is in principle boundless. "There is no anachronism," wrote Leo Spitzer,

> in finding a link between Whitman's lists—*der Katalogdichter*, the poet of the catalogue, as Eulenberg called him—and the great almanacs of assorted goods. *Leaves of Grass* was published in 1855, and it's around this date that the huge development of the bazaars of the West—department stores—began.*

Katalogdichter for an age of conquest and abundance: yes, but not only.

Free verse. "A 'rational demographic composition' is 'naturally' given in America," writes Gramsci in the prison notebook on *Americanismo e Fordismo*, because in the United States

> there are no large classes that don't play an essential role in the world of production—no wholly parasitic classes. The "tradition" of European "civilization" is by contrast characterized precisely by such classes, that are the product of the "wealth" and "complexity" of its long history.†

Baudelaire, aimlessly wandering through Paris looking for inspiration, is a perfect distillation of such classes; but Whitman, writes Rubén Dario in the sonnet "Walt Whitman" (1890), "tells the

---

*Leo Spitzer, "La enumeracion caotica en la poesia moderna," 1945, in *Linguistica y historia literaria*, Greidos, Madrid, 1961, p. 259n.
† Antonio Gramsci, *Quaderni del carcere*, Einaudi, Torino, 1975, p. 2141.

eagle, 'Fly!,' and 'Row!' to the sailor, / And 'work!' to the vigorous labourer."* Fly, row, work . . . Far from being "parasitic," Whitman's Americans are always *doing* something:

> The pure contralto sings in the organ loft,
> The carpenter dresses his plank, the tongue of his
>   foreplane whistles its wild ascending lisp,
> The married and unmarried children ride home to their
>   Thanksgiving dinner,
> The pilot seizes the king-pin, he heaves down with a
>   strong arm,
> The mate stands braced in the whale-boat, lance and
>   harpoon are ready,
> The duck-shooter walks by silent and cautious
>   stretches,
> The deacons are ordain'd with cross'd hands at the
>   altar,
> The spinning-girl retreats and advances to the hum of
>   the big wheel.
>
> **("Song of Myself," 3)**

Contralto, carpenter, children, pilot, mate . . . With each new line, a new character appears: always at the beginning of the verse, and as its grammatical subject. Next comes the verb, telling us what they are all doing ("The contralto *sings*," "The carpenter *dresses*," "The pilot *seizes*"), and then the object ("dresses *his plank*"), or the place and manner of their actions ("sings *in the organ loft*," "heaves down *with a strong arm*"). Subject-verb-predicate: the simplest

---

* "Dice al águila: 'Vuela!'; 'Boga!,' al marino / y 'Trabaja!' al robusto trabajador."

sentences one can imagine. You read, you understand, you move on. You read, you understand—and it's poetry! It's a little miracle: everyday language, "raised" to the status of art. And what makes it all possible is the "free verse" that was Whitman's greatest innovation: free, in the technical sense that it is no longer "bound" by the regular recurrence of rhythmic or phonetic patterns, thus allowing each sentence to take shape with total freedom, unhindered by external constraints. But free *verse*; not prose; we read and, when we reach the end of the line—we pause. We don't continue directly with the next sentence, as we would with prose, and although the pause may be just a moment, it's enough to indicate that, here, the fundamental building block is verse. And in fact the *single* verse: typical of *Leaves of Grass* is how often its lines can stand on their own. A character appears, acts, and that's it. This is *my* verse. I will not expand beyond it, but no one should trespass, either. Perfect complementarity of macro and micro in Whitman's work: just as the catalogue allows the United States to reach a truly epic dimension, the single verse erects an impassable barrier around each individual American. An entire continent—of isolated characters. Leaves, of grass.

American space.   Free also in this, Whitman's verses: that there is no *hierarchy* among them. Each line has exactly the same value as any other, and they all project this formal equality onto the social types they contain: all of them placed democratically on the same level.* It's a space with room for everybody, that of

---

* "The phrase [. . .] provides the fundamental technique Whitman uses to become the poet of democracy," writes Angus Fletcher in *A New Theory for American Poetry*; unlike clauses, which "express superordinate and subordinate relationships [. . .] no phrase is ever *grammatically* [. . .] superior to any

Whitman's catalogues, *as long as all social atoms accept to remain separate*. "Whitman selects occupations that can be presented as self-sufficient," writes David Simpson: "traders, mechanics, farmers, and so forth" all exist "*next* to each other but never interfering or challenging each other."* Next to, but never against: Whitman, David Reynolds has pointed out, feared

> any form of extreme social activism that he thought might rip apart the social fabric [. . .] Facing extremes, he began tentatively testing out statements that balanced opposites, as though rhetorical juxtaposition would dissolve social tensions.†

It was from this balancing of opposites, Reynolds continues, that "the first truly 'Whitmanesque' verses" emerged, in a notebook from 1847: "I am the poet of slaves, and of the masters of slaves . . ." A verse that combines a poetic "I" and a couple of plurals: Whitmanesque, no question about that. But one wonders: Can there really be "a poet of slaves, and of the masters of slaves"? Equidis-

---

other phrase." Angus Fletcher, *A New Theory for American Poetry: Democracy, the Environment, and the Future of Imagination*, Harvard UP, 2004, p. 219.

*David Simpson, "Destiny Made Manifest: The Style of Whitman's Poetry," in Homi K. Bhabha, ed., *Nation and Narration*, Routledge, London and New York, 1990, pp. 188, 182.

†David S. Reynolds, "Politics and Poetry: *Leaves of Grass* and the Social Crisis of the 1850s," in Ezra Greenspan, ed., *The Cambridge Companion to Walt Whitman*, Cambridge UP, 1995, pp. 82–83. "Since the entire scheme was based upon an ideal of all-pervasive and almost promiscuous Union," writes Kenneth Burke, "the motives of secession that culminated in the Civil War necessarily filled him with anguish." Kenneth Burke, "Policy Made Personal—Whitman's Verse and Prose-Salient Traits," 1955, in Edwin Haviland Miller, ed., *A Century of Whitman Criticism*, Indiana UP, Bloomington, 1971, p. 293.

tance from contralto and carpenter, it's easy to understand; in the end, they have nothing to do with each other. Slaves and masters have *everything* to do: How can that verse join them with a simple "and," as if they could coexist without the slightest problem? It can, if poetry is conceived—*and, through poetry, society itself*—as a collection of self-sufficient units, among which there is spatial contiguity, but neither relationships nor conflict (whence, incidentally, Whitman's silence on the massacres of the westward expansion). "Song of Myself," 42:

> Many sweating, ploughing, thrashing, and then the chaff
> for payment receiving;
> A few idly owning, and they the wheat continually
> claiming.

The point, here, is clearly the clash between the "many" and the "few" on the products of labor; but then, why dispatch them into two separate lines? Conflict *binds them together*; versification *separates* them. It doesn't make sense—but it's how Whitman writes: each verse, its own little world. He has created this form, which now turns against him: his politics pulls in one direction, the politics of his form in the opposite one, and the outcome is an embarrassing mess. The same with the swarm of present participles—sweating, ploughing, thrashing, receiving, owning, claiming: six in twenty words!—that is possibly the clumsiest note in the passage. Here, too, there is a reason for what is happening: present participles are perfect for that "chaotic enumeration" (Spitzer) of parallel actions that is typical of *Leaves of Grass*— ". . . *hoeing* rows of carrots and parsnips—*crossing* savannas—*trailing* in forests; / *Prospecting—gold-digging—girdling* the trees of a new purchase . . ." ("Song of Myself," 33)—and are therefore by far Whitman's most distinctive verb form.* But precisely because they are so good at representing what is fluid and indeterminate, present participles are very *bad* at stating in a definite way that an injustice has been consummated. Conclusion is not what they do. Once again, politics clashes with form, and the result is an awkward stalemate. "Just as few poets have ever written better [than Whitman]," observed another American writer, "few poets have ever written worse."† True. And worst of all, is Whitman on conflict.

III

Fait divers. "Mine a word of the modern, the word En-Masse," declares section 23 of "Song of Myself." "Modernity is the transitory, the fugitive, the contingent," echoes in the same years Baudelaire's "Painter of Modern Life."‡ Both writers perceive a historical discontinuity in the world around them, and want to bring this unsung "modern" quality into their poetry. But here the agreement ends. "Singing my days," reads Whitman's "Passage to India,"

---

*On this, see Ezra Greenspan, who speaks of a "lifelong attachment to the grammatical form of the present participle" ("Some Remarks on the Poetics of 'Participle-Loving Whitman,'" in *The Cambridge Companion to Walt Whitman*, cit., p. 92).

† Randall Jarrell, "Some Lines on Whitman," in *Poetry and the Age*, Knopf, New York, 1953, p. 117.

‡ Charles Baudelaire, "Le peintre de la vie moderne," 1863, in Charles Baudelaire, *Oeuvres complètes*, II, Gallimard, Paris, 1976, p. 695. Though the claim that Baudelaire coined the word "modernité" is a legend (others had used it before him), he does seem to have been the first to focus *explicitly* on it (using it, among other things, as the title for the fourth section of his essay).

Singing the strong light works of engineers,
Our modern wonders (the antique ponderous Seven
    outvied)

This is Whitman's modernity: the wonders of progress. Robust; visible. One senses in Paris, writes for his part Baudelaire, "a something which you will allow me to call 'modernity,' for I know no better word to express this idea [. . .] Modernity is the transitory, the fugitive, the contingent . . ." In lieu of the strong work of engineers, it is the *instability* of contemporary life that inspires the "Tableaux Parisiens" ("Parisian Scenes") that, from the 1861 edition on, form the center of *Les fleurs du mal*:

One morning, while in the somber street . . .
("Les sept vieillards")

Deafening, the street around me shrieked . . .
("À une passante")

. . . one morning, at the time when Labor
awakes under a cold clear sky . . .
("Le cygne")*

A day like any other one; a walk without any particular expectation. Then, from the "crisscross of countless connections" that is

---

* "Un matin, cependant que dans la triste rue" ("Les sept vieillards"); "La rue assourdissante autour de moi hurlait" ("À une passante"); ". . . un matin, à l'heure où sous les cieux / Froids et clairs le Travail s'éveille . . ." ("Le cygne"). All quotations from *Les fleurs du mal* are from Charles Baudelaire, *Oeuvres complètes*, I, Gallimard, Paris, 1975; translations are mine.

typical of "enormous cities" like Paris,* the contingent unexpectedly materializes:

> Suddenly, an old man, whose yellowed rags
> Mirrored the color of that rainy sky . . .
> (**"Les sept vieillards"**)

> Tall, slim, in mourning, majestic in sorrow,
> A woman passed by . . .
> (**"À une passante"**)

> There I saw, one morning, at the time when Labor
> awakes under a cold clear sky, and streetsweepers
> raise a dirty tornado in the silent air

> A swan, who had broken out of its cage . . .
> (**"Le cygne"**)†

It is "the unforeseen that appears, the unknown that passes by,"
of one of the most programmatic texts of *Le spleen de Paris*, "The
Crowds": an event so startling, it triggers its own little narrative.
Another contrast with Whitman, whose poetry was profoundly

---

*These words appear in the brief text with which Baudelaire dedicated *Le
spleen de Paris* to Arsène Houssaye: Charles Baudelaire, *Oeuvres complètes*, I,
Gallimard, Paris, 1975, p. 276.

† "Tout à coup, un vieillard dont les guenilles jaunes / Imitaient la couleur de
ce ciel pluvieux" ("Les sept vieillards"); "Longue, mince, en grand deuil, dou-
leur majestueuse, / Une femme passa / [. . .] / Un éclair . . . puis la nuit!—
Fugitive beauté" ("À une passante"); "Là je vis, un matin, à l'heure où sous les
cieux / Froids et clairs le Travail s'éveille, où la voirie / Pousse un sombre
ouragan dans l'air silencieux, / Un cygne qui s'était évadé de sa cage" ("Le
cygne").

anti-narrative: his characters, all bound to a single immutable activity (the contralto singing, the connoisseur looking at paintings, and so on), in that coincidence of person and work celebrated in the "Carol of Occupations." *Leaves of Grass* was the poem of *identity*; of *repetition*, in the strongest sense of the word. In Baudelaire, only the *un*repeatable matters. The strange; the *fait divers*, as nineteenth-century French journalism called it ("news item," in the colorless English translation). *"Divers,"* because the event in question is "different" from those included among the international or national news, in politics, economics, culture, and so on. A residue; a "something" that no category can comprehend. But a powerful residue, with a unique semantic force: which first generates the "panic feeling that signs are everywhere" (Roland Barthes)—and then, by endowing them with an "uncertain content," leaves us absolutely baffled.* Seven identical old men emerging out of nowhere, and marching in the same direction; a swan, right in front of the Louvre. They *must* be signs; but signs of what? The world has been simultaneously re-enchanted (it "speaks" to us again) and turned into an enigma (what is it saying?). And it's all made even more disconcerting by settings that are almost preposterously ordinary: "the somber street," "the new Carousel," "the deafening street," the "din of the omnibus" ("Les petites vieilles"), "the Seine, deserted" ("Crepuscule du matin"). The map of the *fait divers* is a map of modern everyday Paris. But what is modern Paris?

Ghosts. In one of the prose poems of *Le spleen de Paris*, "The Old Acrobat," the narrator is enjoying the "explosion of vitality" of a Paris fairground ("light, dust, calls, joy, tumult"), when suddenly,

---

* Roland Barthes, "Structure of the *Fait-Divers*," 1964, in *Critical Essays*, Northwestern UP, 1972, pp. 191, 194.

in a remote corner, he finds himself face to face with "a ruin of a man": "He had given up, he had abdicated. His destiny was sealed." The narrator is about to leave the old acrobat a few coins, "when a powerful tide of people, caused by some unknown trouble or other, dragged me far away from him."* This is what modern Paris is like: a sudden, collective, inexplicable, irresistible thrust. Leading . . . where? No answer. The seven old men "march in lock-step *towards an unknown aim*." "I ignore *where you run*, you don't know *where I go*" ("À une passante"). The transient, the contingent, the fugitive . . . *especially* the fugitive. In Whitman, the historical acceleration of modernity pointed confidently towards the future:

> Years of the modern! years of the unperform'd!
> Your horizon rises . . .
>
> **("Years of the Modern")**

In Baudelaire, the years of the modern point *away* from the horizon that rises towards what has been left behind instead. After the crowd has separated him from the old acrobat, the narrator remains "obsessed by that vision." Same with the swan—"So, in front of this Louvre, an image still oppresses me: / I think of my great swan . . ."—and with the passerby: "You, whom I would have loved! You, who knew it!" What has been abandoned has become unforgettable. Haussmann's attack on the old city center†—"The old Paris is no more (the form of a city / Changes more quickly, alas, than the heart of us mortals)" ("Les sept

---

* Charles Baudelaire, "Le vieux saltimbanque," in *Le spleen de Paris in Oeuvres complètes*, I, Gallimard, Paris, 1975, p. 296.
† Ten of the eighteen "Tableaux Parisiens" were written between 1857 and 1861—that is to say, after Napoleon III launched his "modernization" of Paris in 1854. Among the poems inspired by the new situation were the master-

vieillards")—has only strengthened the memory of the past: "J'ai plus de souvenirs que si j'avais mille ans" ("Spleen II"). Forget the wonders of engineers; modernity reveals itself *in those it destroys*: "A ruin of a man"; "Ruins! My family!" ("Les petites vieilles": who are also described as "wounded animals.") Figures of defeat: the "bitter laughter / Of the vanquished, filled with sobs and curses" ("Obsession"), which Baudelaire associates with a line from *Prometheus Bound*; the Hope of "Spleen IV" that,

> Defeated, weeps, while heinous, despotic Anxiety
> On my reclining skull raises its black flag.*

These are the inhabitants of modern Paris. Ghosts. "Anthill city, city full of dreams, / Where the ghost in full day grabs the passerby" ("Les sept vieillards"). Paris is becoming modern, *and therefore* is full of ghosts: "Les sept vieillards" and "Les petites vieilles" were first published in the *Revue contemporaine* under the title "Fantômes Parisiens." Ghosts, and exiles:

> Andromache, I think of you
> [. . .]
> I think of the black woman, wasted and tubercular,
> Treading in the mire, searching with haggard eye
> For the palm trees of superb Africa, that are not here
> [. . .]

---

pieces of the collection: "Le cygne," "Les sept vieillards," "Les petites vieilles," and "À une passante."

* "Vaincu, pleure, et l'Angoisse atroce, despotique, / Sur mon crâne incliné plante son drapeau noir."

> Of all those who have lost something that will never be
>   found
> Never, never again!
> [. . .]
> Of orphans, skin and bones, drying up like flowers!
> [. . .]
> I think of sailors, forgotten on an island,
> Of captives, of the defeated . . . and of so many more!
> ("Le cygne")*

It's Baudelaire's version of the catalogue: a dance of death. "The modern, when it was first theoretically articulated—in Baudelaire—bore an ominous aspect," writes Adorno in *Aesthetic Theory*; its formal correlate, being "the immense importance of all dissonance for new art since Baudelaire and *Tristan*—veritably an invariant of the modern."[†] Dissonance and the ominous: true. But what exactly *is* dissonance in the realm of poetry? In music we know. In literature?

Dissonance. Let's begin with a very simple relationship: adjective and noun. In Whitman, the adjective invariably strengthened the core meaning of the noun: the arm was strong, the harpoon ready, the deacons' hands crossed, and so forth. In

---

* "Andromaque, je pense à vous! / [. . .] / Je pense à la négresse, amaigrie et phtisique, / Piétinant dans la boue, et cherchant, l'oeil hagard, / Les cocotiers absents de la superbe Afrique / [. . .] / À quiconque a perdu ce qui ne se retrouve / Jamais, jamais! / [. . .] / Aux maigres orphelins séchant comme des fleurs! / [. . .] / Je pense aux matelots oubliés dans une île, / Aux captifs, aux vaincus! . . . à bien d'autres encor!"

[†] Theodor W. Adorno, *Aesthetic Theory*, 1970, Bloomsbury, London and New York, 2013, pp. 30, 18.

Baudelaire, the adjective works *against* the noun, forcing it into unfamiliar territory: from the "delicate monster" and "hypocritical reader" of "Au lecteur," through "absent chimeras" ("Bohémiens en voyage"), "useless star" (*Avec ses vêtements . . .*"), "foggy Sahara" ("Spleen II"), "ironic sky" ("Le cygne"), "voracious Irony" ("L'héautontimouménos"), "ridiculous hanged man" ("Un voyage à Cythère"), and many more. Baudelaire's was "the genius of impropriety," wrote his arch-enemy, Brunetière, and he was right: *Les fleurs du mal* relishes in semantic discord, which turns into its characteristic style: "great angel with a spider's forehead" (*"Je te donne ces vers . . ."*); "rivers of coal climbing towards the firmament" ("Paysage"); "Anthill city, city full of dreams" ("Les sept vieillards").* On a larger scale:

> *Mysteries flow like sap*, everywhere
> In the narrow canals of the colossus.
>
> **("Les sept vieillards")**[†]

> I think of my great swan, with its crazy gestures,
> *Ridiculous and sublime, as exiles are.*
>
> **("Le cygne")**[‡]

---

*Discussing "Spleen IV" ("Quand le ciel bas et lourd . . ."), Auerbach himself pointed out the many "strangely disfigured" echoes, "startling," "incongruous," and "unsuited" elements, "harsh and painful disharmony," and "incoherent combinations" of the text. ("The Aesthetic Dignity of the *Fleurs du Mal*," 1950, in *Scenes from the Drama of European Literature*, Univ. of Minnesota Press, 1984, pp. 203–204, 208, 213, 215–16, 224–25.)

[†] Les mystères partout coulent comme des sèves / Dans les canaux étroits du colosse puissant.

[‡] Je pense à mon grand cygne, avec ses gestes fous, / Comme les exilés, ridicule et sublime.

All the way to the extreme case of "A carcass," where, from the rotting body of an animal,

> . . . black battalions emerged
> Of maggots, *that streamed like a thick liquid*
>   Along those living rags.
> [. . .]
> And this world emitted a strange music,
>   *Like running water, and wind,*
>   *Or the grain that, rhythmically, a winnower*
> Shakes and stirs with his fan.*

Now, Baudelaire was not alone in writing like this, in nineteenth-century Europe; *Heart of Darkness*, to name just one, is a true *tour de force* of mystifying similes: "like a weary pilgrimage amongst hints . . . like a sluggish beetle crawling . . . like a somber and polished sarcophagus . . ." But in Conrad, difficulty is always justified by the plot of the novella: the narrator is reluctant to admit Europe's oppression of Africa, so he uses all sorts of convolutions to delay the moment of truth; he is trying to see and not to see, and that's what those overstretched similes are for. Eventually, though, the "weary pilgrimage amongst hints" will turn into something much more straightforward: dissonances will be *resolved*. Baudelaire's never are. That's the breakthrough: dissonances have been "emancipated," to use Schönberg's famous expression; by which

---

*D'où sortaient de noirs bataillons / De larves, qui coulaient comme un épais liquide / Le long de ces vivants haillons / [. . .] /Et ce monde rendait une étrange musique, / Comme l'eau courante et le vent, / Ou le grain qu'un vanneur d'un mouvement rythmique / Agite et tourne dans son van.

he meant that they were now to be considered as "comprehensible" as consonances themselves.* A hanged man—rotting, devoured by birds, disemboweled, castrated—is declared to be ridiculous; we are never told why, *and that's the way it should be.* We must accept this enigmatic predication as "comprehensible": take it as the starting point for our interpretation, and see where that leads us. An army of maggots sounds like the wind. An anthill has dreams. The semantic fabric is ripped apart, and it signifies *through* its laceration. Paris is both antlike in its industriousness and metaphysically oneiric; the two sides no longer form a unity—*and it's precisely this disjunction that defines the historical significance of the modern metropolis.* Half beast, half fantasy. This is what dissonance in literature is like. Just like ghosts and exiles, nothing is in its "right" place anymore. "No one felt less at home in Paris than Baudelaire," wrote Walter Benjamin, and one can easily see why.†

---

* "A radical change in compositional technique [. . .] became necessary when there occurred a development which ended in what I call *the emancipation of dissonance,*" declared Schönberg in a lecture at UCLA in 1941; this expression, he added, "refers to its comprehensibility, which is considered equivalent to the consonance's comprehensibility." Arnold Schönberg, "Composition with Twelve Tones (I)," 1941, in *Style and Idea,* 1950, UC Press, 2010, pp. 216–17. "If the phrase 'emancipation of the dissonance' is taken literally," explains Carl Dahlhaus, "it is directed against the need for resolution. Unresolved dissonances were not rare even in tonal music, but they were interpeted as ellipses. The suppressed note of resolution was simply to be assumed [. . .] The emancipation that Schönberg had in mind, on the other hand, means that dependent dissonances are to be reinterpreted as sonorities in their own right. The exception becomes the rule." Carl Dahlhaus, *Schönberg and the New Music,* 1964, Cambridge UP, 1987, p. 131.

† Walter Benjamin, *The Arcades Project,* Harvard UP, 1999, p. 336.

IV

Simplicity. No one felt less at home in Paris than Baudelaire. But:

> I am
> [. . .]
> A Southerner soon as a Northerner, a planter nonchalant
>   and hospitable down by the Oconee I live,
> A Yankee bound my own way . . .
> [. . .]
> At home on Kanadian snow-shoes, or up in the bush, or
>   with fishermen of Newfoundland;
> At home in the fleet of ice-boats, sailing with the rest and
>   tacking;
> At home on the hills of Vermont, or in the woods of
>   Maine, or the Texan ranch . . .
> **("Song of Myself,"** 16)

At home in space, at home in time:

> . . . I do not talk of the beginning or the end.
> There was never any more inception than there is now,
> Nor any more youth or age than there is now,
> And will never be any more perception than there
>   is now,
> Nor any more heaven or hell than there is now.
> **("Song of Myself,"** 3)

Never any more of anything than there is now . . . "America, you have it better," wrote Goethe, a year before dying:

America, you have it better
than our continent, the old one;
you have no crumbling castles,
and no basalts.
[. . .]
Use the present happily!
And if your children write verse
may a lucky fate protect them
from tales of knights, brigands, and ghosts.
("**To the United States**," 1831)

At home in Vermont, in Texas, in a present without ghosts; most important of all, *at home in language*:

I am of old and young, of the foolish as much as the wise;
Regardless of others, ever regardful of others,
Maternal as well as paternal, a child as well as a man,
Stuff'd with the stuff that is coarse, and stuff'd with the
    stuff that is fine . . .
("**Song of Myself**," 16)

"Young," "wise," "maternal," "child," "man," "coarse," "fine" . . . the nineteenth century struggled endlessly over the meaning of terms like these, culminating in a famous essay—Gottlob Frege's "On Sense and Reference"—which pointed out how all of us inevitably associate different ideas with the very same term.* From Baudelaire on, a large part of modern poetry has seen in this semantic disarticulation a great opportunity to accentuate its

---

*See Gottlob Frege, "On Sense and Reference," 1892, in P. Geach and M. Black, eds., *Translations from the Philosophical Writings of Gottlob Frege*, Basil Blackwell, Oxford, 1952.

subjective component, thus amplifying its distance from other discourses. But not Whitman: who kept using his words as if they were perfectly stable and self-evident. "What I tell I tell for precisely what it is," declares the "Preface" to *Leaves of Grass*: "The greatest poet [. . .] bestows on every object or quality its fit proportions neither more nor less [. . .] Nothing is better than simplicity" [8–9]. Telling it for precisely what it is: with language, this is not really possible. But those subject-verb-predicate verses of *Leaves of Grass* reduce the potential for ambiguity as much as poetry can ever hope to; and insofar as a democratic culture needs a widespread agreement on the meaning of words, then *this is its style*. Simplicity. Aristocratic nations don't really have a common language, Tocqueville observed, but in democracies *"tout le monde se sert des mêmes mots"**—and Whitman shows how to do so. Not only can everybody understand his verses (unlike the ridiculous hanged man and the anthill full of dreams); we are also likely *to understand them in the same way*. In terms of critical reception, this refusal to disconnect poetry from ordinary language has had its price; in a work such as Adorno's *Aesthetic Theory*, where Baudelaire's presence is second only to Beethoven's, Whitman is not mentioned at all—not once. But his epic "simplicity" allowed him to exert a major influence over a different literary tradition: Mayakovsky, Neruda, Ginsberg; a poetry that wanted to reach a large public, and that in order to do so emphasized, in various ways, its proximity to other social discourses. Whether poetry will ever again be truly "heard" by contemporary societies, and have a chance at cultural hegemony—this remains seriously in doubt. But if it does, then Whitman will be its Homer.

---

*Alexis de Tocqueville, *De la démocratie en Amérique*, vol. II, 1840, *Oeuvres*, vol. II, Gallimard, Paris, 1992, pp. 579–80.

III

PROSE AND HISTORY IN
"BIG TWO-HEARTED RIVER"

I

Iceberg. The sixteenth chapter of *Death in the Afternoon* (1932) is a detailed examination of the role played by picadors in bullfighting: what kind of horse they should ride, which of the bull's muscles they should or should not try to attack, and so on. Then, suddenly, the topic changes:

> If a writer of prose knows enough of what he is writing about he may omit things that he knows and the reader, if the writer is writing truly enough, will have a feeling of those things as strongly as though the writer had stated them. The dignity of movement of an ice-berg is due to only one-eighth of it being above water.*

---

*Ernest Hemingway, *Death in the Afternoon*, Scribner, New York, 1999, p. 184.

One-eighth above water. In 1946, when Robert Siodmak developed Hemingway's short story "The Killers" (1927) into a full film noir, the events of the original text occupied about nine minutes out of an hour and a half; as it happened, just under one-eighth. So, yes, the iceberg is a good metaphor for Hemingway's writing; yet some questions remain. Given that only a fraction of the story is still visible in the actual text, what should we think of those seven-eighths that the writer "may omit"? And is Hemingway using the right modal verb here—are these things that "may" be omitted, or that *must* be?

Men had grown silent. The opening paragraph of "Big Two-Hearted River" (1925) is a good starting point to discuss Hemingway's stylistic strategy:

> The train went on up the track out of sight, around one of the hills of burnt timber. Nick sat down on the bundle of canvas and bedding the baggage man had pitched out of the door of the baggage car. There was no town, nothing but the rails and the burned-over country. The thirteen saloons that had lined up the one street of Seney had not left a trace. The foundations of the Mansion House hotel stuck up above the ground. The stone was chipped and split by the fire. It was all that was left of the town of Seney. Even the surface had been burned off the ground.*

What has been "omitted" here? Most interpreters answer: the war. We read "there was no town, nothing but the rails and the burned-over country," or "the foundations of the Mansion House hotel stuck up above the ground," and it's difficult not to think of the

---

* Ernest Hemingway, *The Nick Adams Stories*, Scribner, New York, 1981, p. 177.

photographs from Flanders and the Western Front. Nick's arrival in Seney, Michigan—which of course had never been touched by World War I—acquires its haunting power because of historical associations that are simultaneously evoked, and submerged below the surface. Iceberg. But is this really the achievement of "a writer writing truly enough," as *Death in the Afternoon* will put it? "One of the curses of the war is the collision between events and the language available—or thought appropriate—to describe them," wrote Paul Fussell in *The Great War and Modern Memory*: "The presumed inadequacy of language itself to convey the facts about trench warfare is one of the motifs of all who wrote about the war."* And Walter Benjamin, in "The Storyteller":

> Beginning with the First World War, a process became apparent which continues to this day. Wasn't it noticeable at the end of the war that men who returned from the battlefield had grown silent—not richer, but poorer in communicable experience? [. . .] A generation that had gone to school on horse-drawn streetcars now stood under the open sky in a landscape where nothing remained unchanged but the clouds, and, beneath these clouds, in a force field of destructive torrents and explosions, was the tiny, fragile human body.†

Men had grown silent. They were not "omitting" the details of wartime experiences; *they didn't know how to speak of them*. It is against this background that Hemingway's rhetoric of taciturnity

---

*Paul Fussell, *The Great War and Modern Memory*, 1975, Oxford UP, 2013, pp. 169–70.
†Walter Benjamin, "The Storyteller: Observations on the Works of Nikolai Leskov," 1936, in *Selected Writings*, vol. 3, 1935–1938, Harvard UP, 2002, pp. 143–44.

acquires its historical significance: it's a way of writing that takes the soldiers' aphasia as his starting point and *transforms it from a "curse" into a style*. It is the inner mechanism of this transformation— the "how" of literary form, as I wrote in the introduction—that will be the topic of the pages that follow.

Fourteen words. A rhetoric of taciturnity begins with short, clipped sentences—exactly like those Hemingway is famous for. In his early work on quantitative stylistics, Robert Cluett had found an average of about 25 words per sentence for the Hemingway corpus;* the opening sentences of "Big Two-Hearted River" are, however, considerably shorter—13.8 words on average—as are many other passages in the story:

> He came down a hillside covered with stumps into a meadow. At the edge of the meadow flowed the river. Nick was glad to get to the river. He walked upstream through the meadow. His trousers were soaked with the dew as he walked. After the hot day, the dew had come quickly and heavily. The river made no sound. It was too fast and smooth. At the edge of the meadow, before he mounted to a piece of high ground to make camp, Nick looked down the river at the trout rising. They were rising to insects come from the swamp on the other side of the stream when the sun went down. The trout jumped out of water to take them. While Nick walked through the little stretch of meadow alongside the stream, trout had jumped high out of water. Now as he looked down the river, the insects must be set-tling on the surface, for the trout were feeding steadily all down

---

*Robert Cluett, *Prose Style and Critical Reading*, Teachers' College Press, New York, 1976, p. 32.

the stream. As far down the long stretch as he could see, the trout were rising, making circles all down the surface of the water, as though it were starting to rain. [182]

The mean length of these sentences is 14 words, and many are much shorter. He walked upstream through the meadow. The river made no sound. The trout jumped out of water to take them. Short. Just a couple of weeks before the lecture on "Big Two-Hearted River," though, we had discussed a passage from *Ulysses* whose average sentence length, at 6.7 words, was exactly half that of the Hemingway story. The class on Joyce had nothing to do with brevity (it was on the stream of consciousness as a sort of template for twentieth-century socialization), yet *Ulysses*'s syncopated rhythm had been impossible to miss, and now, retrospectively, it made Hemingway's prose look a lot less pointed and nimble than it usually does.* Many of Joyce's sentences were truncated, or

---

*The passage from Joyce was almost exactly the same length as that from Hemingway: 200 words in one case, and 197 in the other. Here it is: "He looked at the cattle, blurred in silver heat. Silverpowdered olivetrees. Quiet long days: pruning ripening. Olives are packed in jars, eh? I have a few left from Andrews. Molly spitting them out. Knows the taste of them now. Oranges in tissue paper packed in crates. Citrons too. Wonder is poor Citron still in Saint Kevin's parade. And Mastiansky with the old cither. Pleasant evenings we had then. Molly in Citron's basketchair. Nice to hold, cool waxen fruit, hold in the hand, lift it to the nostrils and smell the perfume. Like that, heavy, sweet, wild perfume. Always the same, year after year. They fetched high prices too, Moisel told me. Arbutus place: Pleasants street: pleasant old times. Must be without a flaw, he said. Coming all that way: Spain, Gibraltar, Mediterranean, the Levant. Crates lined up on the quayside at Jaffa, chap ticking them off in a book, navvies handling them barefoot in soiled dungarees. There's whatdoyoucallhim out of. How do you? Doesn't see. Chap you know just to salute bit of a bore. His back is like that Norwegian captain's. Wonder if I'll meet him today. Watering cart. To provoke the rain. On earth as it is in heaven." (*Ulysses*, IV, 201–17)

wholly ungrammatical (Citrons too . . . Like that, heavy, sweet, wild perfume . . . To provoke the rain); Hemingway never forgets his inflected verbs, or endangers the structural completeness of his periods. All of a sudden, he looks decorous—stuffy, almost. The same with semantics: Joyce's page is a Harlequin dress that shifts topics every other line (the cultivation of olives, young Molly, their friends Citron and Mastiansky, the trade in oranges, a random passerby, a final fugitive thought about religion); Hemingway's thematic focus is perfectly consistent and stable. Redundancy is the key here: whereas Joyce hardly repeated any of the words he was using, in Hemingway "down" appears seven times, and "he" six: a man and a direction, made perfectly visible. The next three terms, occurring five times each—"meadow," "river," and "trout"—evoke the basic topography of the paragraph (the trout inside the river inside the meadow), while another dozen, that are repeated, respectively, three (Nick, walked, stream, water, rising) and two times (looked, high, jumped, insects, stretch, dew, surface), give the final touches to this scene of a man moving on the ground and looking for fish that are moving in water. A writer may omit things . . . But here Hemingway is not omitting— *he is repeating things.* River-stream-water-stretch-surface; he-Nick-walked-looked; trout-rising-high-jumped-insects . . . There is a lot of glue, in this way of writing; a surplus of semantic echoes that keep the text together—and make it easy to read. The distance from Joyce could not be greater. *Ulysses* had increased "the amount of observable material" to such an extent that the "overtaxed reader" is constantly trying to "reduce [it] to manageable proportions," Wolfgang Iser has written;* and as all readers of

---

*Wolfgang Iser, *The Implied Reader*, Johns Hopkins UP, Baltimore and London, 1974, p. 204.

Ulysses know, it always feels as if such "reduction" betrays the true greatness of the book. With Hemingway, one never needs to reduce anything. And while his short sentences continue to evoke a vaguely Modernist atmosphere, and the silence about the war spreads a haunting mix of presence and absence, redundancy works as a perfect counterweight, making sure that everything is easily understood. The best of both worlds: small challenges— but in "manageable proportions." And manageable, as we will see, is a really good keyword for Hemingway's fictional universe.

Continuous present. From brevity to repetition; from repetition, to the other great Modernist presence in Hemingway's work. Gertrude Stein, "Melanctha":

> "I don't see Melanctha why you should talk like you would kill yourself just because you're blue. I'd never kill myself Melanctha just 'cause I was blue. I'd maybe kill somebody else Melanctha 'cause I was blue, but I'd never kill myself. If I ever killed myself Melanctha it'd be by accident, and if I ever killed myself by accident Melanctha, I'd be awful sorry."*

Amazing stylization of redundancy. Though each sentence adds something to the previous one—"I'd never kill myself . . . I'd maybe kill somebody else . . . it'd be by accident . . . I'd be awful sorry"— the amount of novelty is kept at an absolute minimum, and further undermined by the omnipresence of Melanctha's name and Stein's conditionals (I'd . . . I'd . . . it'd . . . I'd . . .); the point of the passage is not its forward momentum, but the *resistance* of language to all new developments. Characters (and readers) must

---

* Gertrude Stein, *Three Lives*, 1909, Penguin, Harmondsworth, 1990, p. 161.

struggle with words as if they were an obstacle to expression; as if language were the most inert—the most *dead*—of human faculties. It's Stein's stroke of genius: taking a central theme of *Three Lives*—the difficulty of understanding and expressing one's inner state—and conveying it via a style that *duplicates* the problem, making it insoluble. No matter what characters do, language undercuts their efforts:

> Every day now, Jeff seemed to be coming nearer, to be really loving. Every day now, Melanctha poured it all out to him, with more freedom. Every day now, they seemed to be having more and more, both together, of this strong, right feeling. More and more every day now they seemed to know more really, what it was each other one was always feeling. More and more now every day Jeff found in himself, he felt more trusting. More and more every day now, he did not think anything in words about what he was always doing. Every day now more and more Melanctha would let out to Jeff her real, strong feeling. [109]

Is this passage really showing Jeff and Melanctha "coming nearer" each other? That's what the first sentence says, of course—but when the word "more" is repeated twelve times in a few lines (once every ten words, more or less), it no longer suggests change, but only its impossible *slowness*. The same for the formula "every day now" and the verb forms in "-ing," both of which make us feel that the story is marching in place, caught in that "prolonged" or "continuous present" that Stein herself would describe in "Composition as Explanation" [1926].* If one italicizes

---

* "The composition forming around me was a prolonged present. A composition of a prolonged present is a natural composition in the world as it has been

this handful of recurring features, the density of the prose leaps to the eye:

> *Every day now,* Jeff seemed to be *coming* nearer, to be really *loving. Every day now,* Melanctha poured it all out to him, with *more* freedom. *Every day now,* they seemed to be *having more and more,* both together, of this strong, right *feeling. More and more every day now* they seemed to know *more* really, what it was each other one was always *feeling. More and more now every day* Jeff found in himself, he felt *more trusting. More and more every day now,* he did not think anything in words about what he was always *doing. Every day now more and more* Melanctha would let out to Jeff her real, strong *feeling.*

Thus Stein. And if we now do the same thing with the passage from "Big Two-Hearted River" quoted above, italicizing the five terms that are repeated most often (down, he, meadow, river, trout), this is what we get:

> *He* came *down* a hillside covered with stumps into a *meadow.* At the edge of the *meadow* flowed the *river.* Nick was glad to get to the *river. He* walked upstream through the *meadow.* His trousers

---

these thirty years it was more and more a prolonged present. I created then a prolonged present naturally I knew nothing of a continuous present but it came naturally to me to make one, it was simple it was clear to me and nobody knew why it was done like that, I did not myself although naturally to me it was natural. After that I did a book called *The Making of Americans* it is a long book about a thousand pages. Here again it was all so natural to me and more and more complicatedly a continuous present. A continuous present is a continuous present. I made almost a thousand pages of a continuous present." "Composition as Explanation," in Ulla E. Dydo, ed., *A Stein Reader,* Northwestern UP, 1993, p. 498.

were soaked with the dew as *he* walked. After the hot day, the dew had come quickly and heavily. The *river* made no sound. It was too fast and smooth. At the edge of the *meadow,* before *he* mounted to a piece of high ground to make camp, Nick looked *down* the *river* at the *trout* rising. They were rising to insects come from the swamp on the other side of the stream when the sun went *down*. The *trout* jumped out of water to take them. While Nick walked through the little stretch of *meadow* alongside the stream, *trout* had jumped high out of water. Now as *he* looked *down* the river, the insects must be settling on the surface, for the *trout* were feeding steadily all *down* the stream. As far *down* the long stretch as *he* could see, the *trout* were rising, making circles all *down* the surface of the water, as though it were starting to rain.

It's not just that "Big Two-Hearted River" is a lot less repetitive than "Melanctha"; it is that, as redundancy drops down to Hemingway's level, *its function is reversed*: instead of making the text harder to read, it makes it easier. Stein's deliberately opaque adverbs and adverbials (more, now, every day) are replaced by perfectly recognizable objects (river, meadow, trout) that are presented in an orderly succession: meadow and river are repeated four times in the first half of the paragraph, to establish the setting of the scene; then, after the trout "arise" in mid-paragraph, each of them returns only once, while the trout are mentioned four more times. From ecosystem to organism; the focus is narrowed—is *targeted*—towards the ultimate aim of the story. Without being told so explicitly, we understand that Nick has moved steadily across the narrated world, heading towards his prey. It's not a dramatic development, to be sure, but—especially against the background of Stein's inertia—it is absolutely clear. Just as with Joycean brevity,

Hemingway takes the experiments of the early twentieth century as his starting point, and then retreats to a much more "average" position: short sentences—but not as truncated as Joyce's; repetitions—but not as obstinate as Stein's. It's not a matter of cynicism, or of calculation; after all, he *did* include a long stream-of-consciousness section in *A Farewell to Arms*, and it was Stein herself who (fortunately) convinced him to get rid of it. The fact is, Hemingway's talent did not lie in the exploration of formal extremes that was typical of the Modernist temper. It lay in a different direction.

II

Know-how. There is a verb that keeps recurring in "Big Two-Hearted River"—and that isn't exactly obvious, in a writer like Hemingway:

> It could not all be burned. He *knew* that [. . .] He did not need to get his map out. He *knew* where he was by the position of the river [. . .] He *knew* where he wanted to strike the river [. . .] At any time he *knew* he could strike the river by turning off to his left [. . .] He *knew* it could not be more than a mile [. . .] He *knew* it was too hot [. . .] He *knew* the beans and spaghetti were still too hot [. . .] He *knew* it was a small one [. . .] Nick *knew* the trout's teeth would cut through the snell [. . .] Nick *knew* there were trout in each shadow.

Why this fixation with "knowing," in a story of a man going fishing? Gilbert Ryle's famous lecture "Knowing How and Knowing

That" is a good point to start.* For Ryle, "knowing that"—or, more explicitly, "knowing that something is the case" [4]—manifests itself in "thinking" [5], "theoretical citations" [7], "propounding of propositions" [8], "dicta" [8], and the like; it consists of descriptions and explanations, and is therefore necessarily expressed in words. By contrast, "knowing how" requires someone who *"may pro-pound judgments"* but—the shift in modals says it all—*"must work judiciously"* [8–9]. The fundamental modality of the know-how is not words, but actions: "performances" [2]—and more precisely *"practical* performances" [2]—that rely on a type of "intelligence exhibited by deeds, not by [. . .] dicta" [8]. Deeds, not dicta. Nick, setting up his camp:

> With the ax he slit off a bright slab of pine from one of the stumps and split it into pegs for the tent. He wanted them long and solid to hold the ground. With the tent unpacked and spread on the ground, the pack, leaning against a jack pine, looked much smaller. Nick tied the rope that served the tent for a ridgepole to the trunk of one of the pine trees and pulled the tent up off the ground with the other end of the rope and tied it to the other pine. The tent hung on the rope like a canvas blanket on a clothesline. Nick poked a pole he had cut up under the back peak of the canvas and then made it a tent by pegging out the sides. He pegged the sides out taut and drove the pegs deep, hitting them down into the ground with the flat of the ax until the rope loops were buried and the canvas was drum tight. [183]

---

* Gilbert Ryle, "Knowing How and Knowing That," *Proceedings of the Aristotelian Society*, 1945–46, pp. 1–16.

In this eminently "practical performance"—ax, pine, stumps, tent, ground, sack, rope—Nick splits the stump "into pegs *for* the tent"; the pegs must be "long and solid *to* hold the ground"; he drives them down "*until* the rope loops were buried." Though his intentions are never expressed as such, the frequency of final clauses makes all he does extraordinaraily *purposeful*. Without "paying lip-service to rules and principles" (Ryle again), the text shows how the know-how follows an unwritten pattern, in which movements are connected to one another like so many links in a chain. No gesture is wasted or inaccurate; they are all "useful"; done, *in order to do something else*. Time is segmented neatly and without hurry: "he slit off a bright slab [. . .] *and* split it"; "Nick tied the rope [. . .] *and* pulled the tent up [. . .] *and* tied it to the other pine." Every clause is a new step, and only *one* step; every movement, so neatly integrated into what precedes and follows, that we absorb its novelty, without ever being surprised. And one wonders: Why write a story in such a modest, almost self-effacing fashion?

Words and things. Let's have another look at the style of the know-how. This time, Nick is preparing to go fishing:

> Nick took it *from his hook book*, sitting *with the rod* / *across his lap.* He tested the knot and the spring *of the rod* by pulling the line taut. It was a good feeling. He was careful not to let the hook bite *into his finger.*
>
> He started *down to the stream*, holding his rod, the bottle *of grasshoppers* hung *from his neck* / *by a thong* tied *in half hitches* / *around the neck* / *of the bottle.* His landing net hung *by a hook* / *from his belt.* / *Over his shoulder* was a long flour sack tied *at each corner* / *into an ear.* The cord went *over his shoulder.* The sack flapped *against his legs.*

Nick felt awkward and professionally happy *with all his equipment* hanging *from him*. The grasshopper bottle swung *against his chest*. *In his shirt* the breast pockets bulged *against him* / *with the lunch and his fly book*. [190]

Twelve short sentences—and *twenty-five* prepositional phrases, italicized in the passage.* Prepositional phrases tighten the relationships between the elements of a sentence (between Nick's chest, shirt, lunch, and fly book, for instance), and in this respect they are one more way of emphasizing the strict concatenation of Nick's practical performances. This time, though, *the performances have already happened*: in contrast to the forward orientation of the scene of the tent, where Nick was constantly aware of what his next step would be, prepositional phrases tell us what he has *already* done: preparing his lunch, packing it, putting it in the shirt pocket, and so on. Actions are *objectified*, literally: they are no longer presented *as actions*, but as parts of his shirt or pocket. When we read that "the bottle *of grasshoppers* hung *from his neck* / *by a thong* tied *in half hitches* / *around the neck* / *of the bottle*," Nick's past activity (catching the grasshoppers, placing them in the bottle, tying the bottle in a particular way, hanging it from his neck) is still somehow implied in Hemingway's words, but is not really *visible* anymore: it lies submerged, below the surface of the lan-

---

*Hemingway's use of prepositional phrases had already been noticed by Cluett, who, however, did not analyze their function in detail (see *Prose Style and Critical Reading*, cit., pp. 154–57). On prepositional phrases in general, see Biber, Johansson, Leech, Conrad, and Finegan, *Longman Grammar of Spoken and Written English*, Pearson, Harlow, 1999, pp. 763–812. Incidentally, the opening sentence of "Big Two-Hearted River" is a sort of *nec plus ultra* of this grammatical construction: "The train *went on* / *up the track* / *out of sight*, / *around one of the hills* / *of burnt timber*."

guage, like the seven-eighths of the iceberg. There has been a (little) story here, but it is no longer presented *as* a story. And so, once more, we encounter the same question: Why all this narrative prudence, on Hemingway's part? After the slow modulation of his thematic focus (from meadow and river to trout, with all that lay in between), and after the "judicious," one-step-at-a-time performances of the know-how—two conventions that had kept under control the forward movement of his story—prepositional phrases extend his circumspection even *backwards in time*. But why? "Every form is the resolution of a fundamental dissonance of existence," wrote Lukács in *Theory of the Novel*.* Good. What, then, is the dissonance Hemingway is trying to resolve—and why does he do it in such an odd way?

Nothing could touch him. "In dealing with a 'war literature,'" Eric Leed has observed, "one is dealing with the testimony of men who, as a rule, had little or no control over the events which threatened their lives."† No control: this is the key. Hemingway's style is *all about control*: of one's movements, time, environment, tools. After the terrifying disproportion between the power of military technology and Benjamin's "tiny, fragile human body," his prose creates a world where the human body returns to be the measure of things. All Nick has is an ax, a rope, a piece of canvas, and a fishing line: even Robinson Crusoe had more. But having so little allows him to feel that all he does is truly his own—and to perceive *time* as his own, too. Life in the trenches had fluctuated frantically between long stretches of boredom and short moments of terror; Hemingway's style doesn't fluctuate at all: orderly and consistent

---

* György Lukács, *Theory of the Novel*, cit., p. 62.
† Eric J. Leed, *No Man's Land*, Cambridge UP, 1981, p. 33.

and uninterrupted, it establishes a cautious sense of the "present": a short bridge leading from the recent past of prepositional phrases to the immediate future of final clauses. Prudence, again; *convalescence* (in a few years, the center of Hemingway's first great success, *A Farewell to Arms*).* And as is often the case in convalescence, the narrowness of one's horizon is felt not as a constraint, but as a source of comfort:

> Across the open mouth of the tent Nick fixed cheesecloth to keep out mosquitoes. He crawled inside under the mosquito bar with various things from the pack to put at the head of the bed under the slant of the canvas. Inside the tent the light came through the brown canvas. Already there was something mysterious and homelike. Nick was happy as he crawled inside the tent . . . [184]

Fixed, keep out, crawled, under the slant, homelike, happy as he crawled . . . "The happiness in what is bound and limited," wrote Roland Barthes in one of his *Mythologies*, "is typical of children's passion for huts and tents."† Children: in the trenches, soldiers assumed a fetal position as "protection" against artillery fire. Nick's tent has a similar function:

---

*Trout fishing is *perfect* for convalescence, combining as it does a total absence of risk with that dose of uncertainty—"The line went slack and Nick thought the trout was gone. Then he saw him . . ."—which is indispensable to keep a story going. Marlins, sharks, bulls, and elephants will eventually provide a headier mix of technical know-how (to keep danger under control) and unpredictable animal power (to rapidly increase narrative tension).

† Roland Barthes, "*Nautilus* and *Bateau ivre*," in *Mythologies*, 1957, Farrar, Straus and Giroux, New York, 1990, p. 65.

. . . Nick was happy as he crawled inside the tent. He had not been unhappy all day. This was different though. Now things were done. There had been this to do. Now it was done. It had been a hard trip. He was very tired. That was done. He had made his camp. He was settled. Nothing could touch him. [184]

Nothing could touch him. Photographs of the Anglo-Boer war, a generation earlier, show encampments formed of long and tidy rows of tents: which is where soldiers used to sleep, before being thrown into the trenches, and exposed to the "force field of destructive torrents" described by Benjamin. A sheet of canvas is of course only a symbolic protection from bombs and gas; but symbols—and magic—became incredibly powerful during World War I. Hemingway's prose style is part of that magic; a sort of retrospective exorcism of an unspeakable trauma. He had made his camp. He was settled. Nothing could touch him.

DAY AND NIGHT: ON THE COUNTERPOINT
OF WESTERN AND FILM NOIR

Day and night. Figure 2: John Ford's stagecoach is on its way; we see the uneven terrain, the buttes of Monument Valley, the horizon, the clouds in the sky (*Stagecoach*, 1939). It's the long shot of the Western: a way of filming that turns the landscape into the protagonist of the story; a space so vast, it dwarfs the human beings within it; the empty, "alien" space of the Frontier, "which had been in its time as uncanny a place for pioneers as a moonscape might be."* Figure 3: Barbara Stanwyck and Fred MacMurray are planning their next moves in *Double Indemnity* (1944); it's the urban, everyday setting of a supermarket; customers walk by, a woman gets some baby formula, a janitor pushes a cart; boxes, cans, stuff everywhere; a crowded space, made even more so by the close-up characteristic of film noir. But proximity doesn't bring clarity: Stanwyck's sunglasses make her expression com-

---

*Richard Slotkin, *Gunfighter Nation: The Myth of the Frontier in Twentieth-Century America*, Univ. of Oklahoma Press, 1992, p. 305.

Figure 2.

Figure 3.

pletely unreadable (and it doesn't get better when, later, she takes them off). In the Western, the opposite state of affairs: distance makes it often difficult to see—all those characters knitting their brows and shielding their eyes, trying to make sense of the figures moving against the horizon—but it never generates *ambiguity*; one either sees, or doesn't. Daylight; *High Noon*; a genre *en plein air*, eager for color, which it embraced as soon as it became technically available. Not so the noir, whose passion for darkness— *Nightfall, Black Angel, Gaslight, The Night of the Hunter, The Dark Corner* . . . —remained firmly committed to the thousand gradations of black-and-white film.* They are contemporary, these two great postwar genres; and they are antithetical, too. This chapter examines their opposition, and reflects on its historical significance.

I

West. Initially, there was no such thing as "the Western": the word was just an adjective that added some local color to a variety of genres ranging from "Western comedies" to "Western melodramas," "chase films," "romances," and "epics."† But the adjective was a geographical one, and it quickly overshadowed the nouns it was supposed to serve, because geography was essential to the

---

* "A little strange, to see the old place in the daytime," muses Burt Lancaster in *Criss-Cross* (1949). It's the same feeling one has while watching *Murder by Contract* (1958), with its odd relish for daylight and the outdoor. "You want to see the location [of the planned murder], don't you?" asks the killer's driver as they are cruising around Los Angeles in a convertible. "Not today" is the answer: "It's too nice today. Can't be bothered with stuff like that."

† Rick Altman, *Film Genre*, British Film Institute, London, 1999, p. 36.

new form. Think of the titles: rivers (*Red River, Rio Bravo, Rio Grande* . . .); states and other large regions (*The Virginian, Texas Rangers, Nevada Smith, California, Cimarron* . . .); outposts (*Fort Apache, The Alamo, Comanche Station* . . .); a few cities (*Vera Cruz, 3:10 to Yuma, San Antonio, The Man from Laramie* . . .); plus an entire lexicon of space and movement (*The Big Trail, Destry Rides Again, Stagecoach, The Bend in the River, Two Rode Together, Canyon Passage* . . .). Every story needs a space in which to unfold, of course, but the Western does more; it is in love with space; it foregrounds it, full-screen, whenever it can. The start of the cattle drive in *Red River* (1948): in two minutes, we get a static background (drovers and herd, at dawn, motionless against the landscape), a panoramic so powerful—this is our cattle, this is our land—not even a legendary continuity blunder can spoil it,* a confident sense of direction ("Take them to Missouri, Matt"), and an explosion of joy.† Beginnings are particularly good at evoking the immensity of this space: in *The Man of the West* (1958), a horseman appears on the horizon, looks at the empty expanse around him, and rides calmly off; in *The Virginian* (1929) and *My*

---

*Given the initial position of the camera, the shot cannot possibly end—as it does—on John Wayne's right side. But it doesn't matter.

†Though *Red River* moves north (from Texas to Kansas, and then to Missouri), the genre's sense of direction is obviously westward (there is even a John Wayne *Westward Ho*, unrelated to the novel of Elizabethan expansion), in a movement that shifts the baricenter of American identity farther and farther away from the Old World; in the Tombstone of *My Darling Clementine* (1946), the drunk actor no longer remembers "To be or not to be" (and Doc Holliday, who does, is silenced by a fit of coughing). Tellingly, the westward movement tends to stop before reaching the Pacific, as its unpassable expanse would dampen the genre's expansionist energy; as a result, even scenes that take place in its waters (such as the opening of *The Far Country*, 1954) are shot in such a way as to make the ocean almost invisible.

Darling Clementine, a herd of cows disperses slowly in every direction; in *Red River, The Man from Laramie* (1955), and *Rio Bravo* (1959), it's wagons that advance cautiously this way and that. Cautiously, slowly, calmly: the initial tempo of the Western: *Lento assai*. The first ten minutes of *Once Upon a Time in the West* (1968): three men at a station, a fly buzzing, a wheel screeching, a drop of water hitting the rim of a hat. In no other form does *waiting*—for the train, the attack, the night, the stage, the cavalry . . . —play such a large role: a dilated sense of time, mirroring the enlargement of space. *The Big Trail, The Big Sky, The Big Country*. Big, and empty: in film after film, the first to "set eyes" on the land is a white man, *who sees nothing but an uninhabited country*. Native Americans—"Indians," as the Western calls them—were of course already living in the West (and everywhere else in America, for that matter); but by routinely introducing them only *after* we have already become familiar with white characters, the Western makes them look like illegitimate intruders. In reality, they were there first; in fiction, they arrive always too late. Seldom has narrative lied so spectacularly about the history it claimed to narrate.

Wagon train. "Cinema is the specifically epic art," wrote André Bazin in a famous essay on American film, and "the migration to the West is our *Odyssey*."* Epic, yes; *Odyssey*, no. That there is no return is the founding act of the genre. Home is a vague hope, distant in space and in time; for now, all there is is a wagon; two or three generations, together, surrounded by hundreds of other families; all different, and all leading exactly the same life. Life in the open, on unsteadily undulating stoops, under everybody's eyes;

---

*André Bazin, "The Western, or the American Film Par Excellence," 1953, in *What Is Cinema?*, vol. II, UC Press, 1971, p. 148.

because what matters, in these films, is not the private sphere of the individual family—we never see the inside of a wagon, and the intimacy of a sentimental conversation, or of a good wash, are often met with rough collective humor—but the amalgamation of everybody into a community. Into a nation. "Gathered from the North, the South and the East, they assemble on the bank of the Mississippi for the conquest of the West," announces the opening of *The Big Trail* (1930).* Conquest: the tempo remains slow, but it has become unyielding. The eyes of the American people, wrote Tocqueville at the onset of the great migration, "are fixed upon [their] own march across these wilds, draining swamps, turning the course of rivers, peopling solitudes, and subduing nature"; they "enjoy dreaming about what will be."† Dreaming . . . But this is more like an obsession. The march of the wagon train can never stop: a hasty prayer, and the dead are buried and left forever behind; a child is born, and hours later is already on the move. Everyday life is both implacably everyday—always brewing coffee, always mending socks and washing their only passable shirt—and frightfully unpredictable: a danger that comes less from human enemies (although the conflict with "Indians" is present in most films of migration), than from the hostility of nature: it's always too hot, too cold, too dry, too windy . . . rain, dust, snow, mountains, rapids . . .‡ So much *friction*, in these films: not a journey in

---

* "We're blazing a trail that started in England!" cries the scout in the same film, as the wagon train has stopped at the foot of the Rockies and is losing hope of ever reaching its destination: "Not even storms of the sea could turn back those first settlers [. . .] Famine, hunger—not even massacres could stop them [. . .] We're building a nation!"

† Alexis de Tocqueville, *De la démocratie en Amérique*, cit., pp. 586–87.

‡ Displacing the main conflict from "Indians" to nature is another way of presenting the conquest of the West in a fundamentally innocent light. Just like Africans in colonial romances (a late nineteenth-century genre virtually

which a wagon doesn't get stuck in the mud; not a scene in which they go *downhill*, for a change. Rarely do fictional characters work as hard as in early Westerns: keeping the animals together, cutting down trees, crossing rivers, digging passages, overcoming crazy obstacles. After all this, they *deserve* the West.* They have been a stubborn, single-minded human herd; which is the reason *Red River*, with its supremely unpromising storyline (moving ten thousand cows from Texas to Missouri, imagine that), is the greatest of all epic Westerns. Those cattle are the settlers: and in the film's terrifying stampede, caused by a man who wants to eat sugar in the middle of the night, the destructive potential of the great migration erupts for a moment, earthquake-like, into the open.

Seven. The wagon train is an early figure in the history of the Western; eventually, the genre leaves the plains for the towns of *My Darling Clementine*, *High Noon*, or *Rio Bravo*. Somewhere in between, lies the great hybrid of *Stagecoach*: a film that moves from

---

contemporary to the Western), "Indians" are made to blend with the American natural landscape, until they are almost identified with it: smoke signals arising from a distant rock, bird calls echoing through the night, bodies barely discernible behind moving branches, the war party emerging as if from nowhere along the ridge . . . From *Stagecoach* to *The Stalking Moon* (1968), there is a chthonic quality to the existence of "Indians": at once primeval, terrifying, and doomed.

* The chapter "Of Property" in Locke's *Second Treatise* (1690)—with its claim that "labour hath taken [land] out of the hands of nature, where it was common, and belong'd equally to all her children, and hath thereby appropriated it to himself"—offered a perfect argument to legitimize the settlers' expropriation of Native Americans. This is also why the latter are routinely presented as hunters—that is to say, as people who do not work the land—while their agricultural civilization is downplayed, or ignored altogether.

one town to another, declares them both unlivable,* and then concentrates on the microcosm of Frontier society that chance has assembled together for the journey. Seven passengers, in the stage's cramped public space: an escaped convict; an alcoholic doctor; a prostitute; a Southern ex-rebel and gambler; a corrupt banker; a wife hiding her pregnancy; and, the most "normal" of them all, a whiskey drummer. As if he were running some sort of experiment, Ford slowly raises the temperature around his passengers, and a memorable series of staccato one-minute scenes—framed by external shots of the stagecoach racing through Monument Valley, as if to remind us of the pressure they are under—shows the seven characters clashing over and over again.† During the last of these exchanges, the doctor makes explicit how implausible their encounter has been from the start: "Ladies and gentlemen, since it's most unlikely that we'll ever have the pleasure of meeting again socially . . ." Then an arrow whistles through the

---

*The first town, Tonto, is small, bigoted, and intolerant; the second, Lordsburg, is large, lawless, and brutal. Since five of the seven passengers (banker, doctor, prostitute, gambler, salesman) can do their job only in an urban context, Ford's representation of the towns is particularly striking.

† The doctor and the gambler clash on the Civil War ("the war of the Rebellion . . ." "You mean the war for the Southern Confederacy, sir!" "I mean nothing of the kind!"), and on the ambiguity of the term "gentleman." The banker, Gatewood, who is running away with all of the bank's deposits, expresses his loathing for "the notorious Ringo Kid," who is sitting next to him, while the doctor and the whiskey drummer provide a melancholy subplot of drunken helplessness. The two women—the Lady and the Whore—remain mostly silent, adding the drama of glances to the contest of words. Revealingly, the only one who feels entitled to address the group as a whole, as if he alone could speak for some kind of "general interest," is the banker: "America for Americans! Don't let the government meddle with business! Reduce taxes! Our national debt is shocking!"—all the way to his final prophecy: "What the country needs is a businessman for president!"

air, and the fight against the Apaches brings the seven together for a few minutes. Once the threat is gone, they part once and for all: the gambler has died; the whiskey drummer is taken to the hospital; the banker is arrested by the town marshal; the doctor makes his way to the saloon; the new mother joins her husband in the cavalry; the young prostitute prepares to return to her brothel, while Ringo proceeds to the shootout with the gang that has murdered his brother. Then Ringo survives, and takes her with him to his ranch "across the border," in a Mexico we have never seen; but the real ending had come a few minutes earlier, with the disintegration of the stagecoach seven as a possible metaphor of the Frontier.

Town tamer. Vast landscapes and solitary characters: one watches these openings and is reminded of Whitman's long catalogues of freestanding vignettes: "The duck-shooter walks by silent and cautious stretches, / The deacons are ordain'd with cross'd hands at the altar, / The spinning-girl retreats and advances . . ." Social parataxis: one character next to the other, with as little interference as possible. Space for all: a promise so simple and powerful, it still echoes as the prelude to *Death of a Salesman* ("A melody is heard, played upon a flute. It is small and fine, *telling of grass and trees and the horizon.* The curtain rises."). But the promise is not kept; Westerns are stories of weapons, of death— of killing. "Indians," in the early phase; then mostly white outlaws. Whether acting on their own (Liberty Valance, Jesse James, the Luke Plummer and Frank Miller of *Stagecoach* and *High Noon*) or hired by cattle barons and other monopolistic figures (such as Jack Palance in *Shane*, 1953, or the gang of Judge Gannon in *The Far Country*), outlaws prove that—no matter how wide the "big country" may be—there is never space for all, and the moment comes when conflict becomes unavoidable. At that point, usually, a town meeting is called. In *High Noon*, it takes place in the town's church, interrupting the service; twelve people—twelve: like a jury, or the apostles—express their conflicting opinions, including a woman (the bravest of them all), the priest, and the marshal's best friend, who will end up betraying him. Similar scenes occur in *Man with the Gun*, *Warlock*, *The Magnificent Seven*, *Shane* (the gathering in Van Heflin's cabin), and even *Stagecoach* (the passengers voting on whether to proceed with the journey). These are strangely reflective episodes, for the Western; people reason, listen, argue, try to persuade each other. There is a palpably "democratic" atmosphere: women vote—even prostitutes— well in advance of political history. But their ultimate meaning lies in the *impotence* they project over democratic discussion. Townspeople talk, but will not arm themselves,* and the silence of the man with the gun, standing alone, apart from the rest, is a scathing comment on their verbosity. In terms of values, it is the moment of truth: the moment of violence. "Why does the Western have such a hold on our imagination?" asked Robert Warshow in his "Movie Chronicle"; chiefly, he answered, it's because "it offers a serious orientation to the problem of violence such as can be found almost nowhere else in our culture. One of the well-known peculiarities of modern civilized opinion is its refusal to acknowledge the value of violence. This refusal is a virtue, but like many virtues it involves a certain willful blindness and it encourages hypocrisy."† "My hunch is there won't be any trouble,"

---

* A striking exception is the ending of *The Far Country*, where an entire mining outpost rises up in arms—Fuenteovejuna-like—against the corrupt judge and his hoodlums.

† Robert Warshow, "Movie Chronicle: The Westerner," in *The Immediate Experience: Movies, Comics, Theatre & Other Aspects of Popular Culture*, 1962, enlarged edition, Harvard UP, 2002, p. 121.

declares a character in *High Noon*: "Not one bit." No trouble—when four gunmen are in town to kill the marshal? This is the blindness Warshow had in mind. Time and again, the Western contrasts it with the reality of violence: someone steals cattle, or robs farmers and miners of their land; then threatens them; then kills. And so, sooner or later, violence has to be accepted, not just as an aspect of social life, *but as its very foundation*. "Gentlemen. I'm puttin' the proposition to a vote—namely, to employ Clint Tollinger in the capacity of a town tamer" (*Man with the Gun*). Town tamer: not marshal; someone paid to shed plenty of blood, as if the townspeople were infected by an unknown disorder ("I've seen some cures be harder than the disease," comments the town doctor: "Believe me: his medicine is hard to take, and harder to keep down"). *High Noon*: the young Quaker wife picks up a gun and shoots one of the outlaws in the back, while he is reloading and cannot return fire. We don't see her face while she is shooting. What will her life be, from now on? What would it have been, had she *not* shot the man who was trying to kill her husband?

Legitimate use of physical force. "What is distinctively 'American' is not necessarily the amount or kind of violence that characterizes our history," Richard Slotkin has written, "but the mythic significance we have assigned to [it], and the political uses to which we put that symbolism."* In the Western, this political use consists in making a certain kind of violence feel *legitimate*. Legitimate, first of all because contained—as in these films' most stylized scene: the shootout. Conflict becomes geometry: friend and foe, one in front of the other, with nothing in between, advancing in a

---

* Richard Slotkin, *Gunfighter Nation*, cit., p. 309.

Figure 4.

straight line while looking into each other's eyes (Figure 4).* Distance is stylized, too: not too far, and not too close; two men moving slowly towards each other—John Wayne's and Henry Fonda's main acting feature: the way they *walk*—as if to measure the

---

*Here, too, fiction is the exact reversal of historical reality: "From the documents of western law enforcers," Stefano Rosso has pointed out, "we learn that the autopsies of firearms victims demonstrated that the bullet's entry hole was generally in the back of the body [. . .] Wild Bill Hickok was killed with a bullet in the back of his head in Deadwood in 1876; Jesse James was shot in the back of his head while he was adjusting a picture on the wall in his house in 1882 [. . .] Wyatt Earp and Doc Holliday died in their beds, and Kit Carson in the quarters of his doctor." Stefano Rosso, "The Winning of the Western: Early Dissemination of a Literary Genre," in Marina Dossena and Stefano Rosso, eds., *Knowledge Dissemination in the Long Nineteenth Century*, Cambridge Scholars, Newcastle upon Tyne, 2016, pp. 37–38.

exact spot where shooting can start. It's a dance. In film noir, one is shot from a few inches away, or with the gun's barrel touching the body, like Stanwyck in *The Strange Love of Martha Ivers* (1946), or Mitchum in *Out of the Past* (1947): an index of these films' deadly mix of intimacy and treachery. In the Western, shooters are twenty or thirty steps apart; a *public* dimension, in the town's main street, at midday. The townspeople are present, though usually invisible; hidden indoors, they are waiting to see who will end up ruling the town. Waiting for the realization of Weber's definition of the state: "a human community that (successfully) claims the *monopoly of the legitimate use of physical force* within a given territory."* It's the Western as a political foundation myth: the genesis of the state. ("Where you come from they have policemen and courts and jails to enforce the law. Here, we got nothing": *The Virginian*.) What exactly makes a certain kind of violence legitimate, these films never actually say; and their heroes, who "explain" their conduct by declaring it inevitable ("I have to stay": *High Noon*; "Somebody always stays": *Garden of Evil*, 1954; "Ruby, I ain't got the time to argue the point with you": *Decision at Sundown*, 1957), also don't help. Fundamentally, violence is justified less by arguments than by its restraint: the Westerner is the man who never draws first; who reacts, but never initiates. If he shoots, it's always ultimately in self-defense. It's a behavior that aligns him with the knight of chivalric romances, with his never-ending crusade against the forces of evil; and the Westerner's aimless wandering—Shane, appearing out of nowhere at the beginning of the film, and vanishing into the distance at the end—is itself a muted version of the knight's *quête de l'aventure*. But almost every-

---

*Max Weber, "Politics as a Vocation," 1919, in H. H. Gerth and C. Wright Mills, eds., *From Max Weber*, cit., p. 78.

thing is muted, in these modern knights: the shootout is a less bloody replica of the sword-and-shield duel, just as the adultery of courtly romance morphs into the absence (or death) of the love object; and of course, in lieu of haughty aristocratic beauty, we get the plebeian plainness of a John Wayne. The Old World's conventions are adapted to modern America—and then re-exported triumphantly back into Europe. But on this, more later.

II

Shadows. Film noir also began as an adjective, used in France for the (mostly American) crime novels of the *Série Noire*; and then, beginning in 1946, for films that combined a mystery plot with a pervasive naturalist hopelessness. Noir: shadows. Stanwyck paces back and forth in front of MacMurray, and with her walks her double, stamped on the wall (Figure 5); changing shape, disappearing briefly, at times even splitting into *two* doubles. In *The Third Man* (1949), someone turns on a lamp near a window, and Orson Welles—who had died before the beginning of the film, and had been buried in front of our eyes—materializes from a dark awning; a shadow, brought back to life (Figure 6). Later, as Joseph Cotten and the occupation powers are waiting for him to show up at a rendezvous at night, all of Vienna turns into a city of shadows: statues, soldiers, alleys, and the unfathomable giant—a clear homage to expressionism—that turns out to be a harmless old balloon peddler.* Shadows harden Clifton Webb's features in *The*

---

*Murnau, Lang, and Arthur Robison's programmatic *Schatten* (1923) had immediately made clear the role shadows could play in film. In Italy, one of Rome's earliest movie theaters was called Lux et Umbra.

Figure 5.

Dark Corner (1946), and soften Jane Greer's in *Out of the Past* (1947: "And then I saw her, coming out of the sun. And I knew I wouldn't care about those forty grand."). Shadows intensify our perception of the world, by presenting everything in an equivocal light; they pervade the noir's visual aesthetics in the same way ambiguity permeates its language. Here, too, titles are a good index of the genre's perspective on the world: vaguely threatening metaphors (*Whirlpool, Nightfall, Vertigo, Impact, Blast of Silence*—and, to be sure, *Double Indemnity*);* an enigmatic use of the definite article

---

* "Look, baby, there's a clause in every accident policy," MacMurray explains, "a little something called double indemnity. The insurance companies put it in as a sort of come-on for the customers. It means they pay double on certain accidents. The kind that almost never happen." That the clause needs to be

Figure 6.

(*The Naked Kiss, The Third Man, The Dark Corner, The Clay Pigeon* . . . which corner? what pigeon?); and plenty of allusions to unintelligible events: *The Postman Always Rings Twice, Ride the Pink Horse, Where the Sidewalk Ends, They Live by Night.* In this company, *Dial "M" for Murder* and *Kiss Tomorrow Goodbye* sound refreshingly straightforward.

Magic Mirror Maze. Though just as haunted by death and killing as the Western, the linear geometry of the duel is unthinkable in film noir. *The Lady from Shanghai* places Hayworth and Welles

---

explained to someone as sharp and calculating as Stanwyck suggests that very few people were aware of this "little something" before Wilder's film.

face to face, looking straight into each other's eyes; a few seconds, and a third person emerges from his words ("I thought it was *your husband* you wanted to kill"), to be immediately multiplied by hers ("*George* was supposed to take care of *Arthur*, but he lost his silly head and shot *Broome*"). They are alone—but they are not; someone else is always between them. A few more seconds, and "Arthur" (Hayworth's husband, played by Everett Sloane) shows up in person. Now it is *he* and Hayworth who face each other, guns in their hands; but in the "Magic Mirror Maze" where the scene is set, optics are deceptive: in a particularly baroque moment, Hayworth is aiming straight at the audience, Sloane diagonally, in the same general direction, but also—reflected as he is from several different angles—seemingly at himself (Figure 7): "You'd be foolish to fire that gun. With these mirrors it's difficult to tell. You are aiming at me, aren't you? I'm aiming at you, lover." As they start firing, and glass shatters everywhere, it's impossible to say what is happening to whom (at a certain point, it even looks as if Welles is the one being hit); and even after Hayworth and Sloane die, we are left with the baffling memory of a shootout that adds a third person to the usual two. (The unlikeliness of this situation is the secret behind *The Man Who Shot Liberty Valance*, 1962.) But in fact, triangulation is as essential to the structure of the noir as the binary logic was to the Western. It's the triangle of adultery, of course, as indeed in *The Lady from Shanghai*, or in George Macready's toast "to the three of us"—himself; his wife, Hayworth (always her); and her secret ex-lover, Glenn Ford—in *Gilda* (1946).*

---

*During their first meeting, Macready and Ford had already drunk "to the three of us," including in their toast Macready's "little friend" (a cane with a blade hidden inside). With Hayworth around, the associations are inevitably of a different kind.

Figure 7.

But beyond adultery, what emerges here is the fundamental figure of the social universe of the film noir: the Third.

The Third. "The appearance of the third party," writes Simmel
in the chapter "Sociological Significance of the Third Element" of
his *Sociology*, "indicates transition, conciliation, and abandonment
of absolute contrasts."* The Third can mediate, and act as an im-
partial referee; it stands for all sorts of institutions that mitigate
conflicts and strengthen the social bond. And it's all true—just
not in film noir. Here, the Third *multiplies* conflicts, endlessly
postponing their resolution. "Just don't get too complicated,

---

*Kurt H. Wolff, ed., *The Sociology of Georg Simmel*, The Free Press, Glencoe,
1950, p. 145.

Eddie. When a man gets too complicated, he's unhappy. And when he's unhappy, his luck runs out" (*The Blue Dahlia*, 1946). But things always get too complicated here. Robert Mitchum, addressing Kirk Douglas and Jane Greer in *Out of the Past*:

> "All right, *you* take the frame off *me*. *You* pin the *Eels* murder on *Joe* [. . .] *You* will be happier if you let the cops have *her* [. . .] Some-body's got to take the rap for *Fisher's* murder [. . .] Besides, it's not a frame. *She* shot *him*."
>
> "*I'*ll say *you* killed *him*. *They* will believe *me*."
>
> "Do *you* believe *her*?"

You, me, Eels, Joe, her, somebody, Fisher, they . . . The adulterous triangle is merely the starting point for an incessant proliferation of corpses. *Double Indemnity*:

> "*You* got *me* to take care of *your husband*, and then you got Zach-etti to take care of *Lola*, and maybe take care of me, too, and then *somebody else* would have come along to take care of Zach-etti for you. That's the way you operate, isn't it, baby."

In the Western, killing was *definitive*: it arose from the discovery of the fundamental conflict, and then—once the enemy was dead—the story was over, and the future could begin. In the noir, killing is just the first step in a series of ever-shifting alliances dictated by the interest of the moment: Stanwick and MacMurray against her husband; Stanwyck and Zachetti against MacMurray; Stanwyck and "somebody else" against Zachetti . . .* It's a multi-

---

*In a sort of virtuoso play with this situation, an endless chain of Thirds is evoked by Kirk Douglas, Stanwyck's husband, in *The Strange Love of Martha*

plication of narrative forces that goes back to the great metropolitan novels by Balzac and Dickens*—and in fact even further back, to Hegel's description of "civil" or "bourgeois" society (the German *"bürgerlich"* encompasses both), in the *Philosophy of Right*:

> In civil society each individual is his own end, all else means nothing to him. But he cannot accomplish the full extent of his ends without reference to others; these others are therefore means to the end of the particular [person] [. . .] The whole [of civil society] is the territory of mediation.†

In this territory of mediation, *using* others—turning them into the means for one's own end—is a much better strategy than simply eliminating them (as was the case in the more rudimentary universe of the Western). In the process, the border between legal and illegal becomes blurry,‡ and narrative structure is placed on an

---

Ivers: "Her life was so empty. Is that what she told you, Sam? [. . .] Now you're all of them, Sam. Every one of them rolled into one [. . .] You're a gymnasium instructor in Philadelphia, with a muscle for a brain and a tendency to insipid verse. You're a guy, just a guy, named Pete, in Erie, who smells of fish and sings. You're last year's greatest fullback . . . and you flunked your bar exam, but you wanted to be an industrial engineer. You're a guy who came along to fix a tire . . . so well you became a city-paid inspector. And you're a lot of others. But worst of all, you're the one and only man who shares with me . . . the only claim I have on her. Ask her, Sam. Say to her, 'Martha, is all this true?'"

*On this, see my *Atlas of the European Novel 1800–1900*, Verso, London, 1998, especially pp. 105–110.

†G. W. F. Hegel, *Elements of the Philosophy of Right*, 1821, Cambridge UP, 1991, p. 220.

‡"None of these men are criminals in the usual sense. They've all got jobs, they all live seemingly normal, decent lives, but they got their problems and they've all got a little larceny in 'em": *The Killing*.

inflationary path: it's always possible to persuade someone to do something they'd never thought of; always possible to add one more character (and another, and another . . .), endlessly expanding the "middle" of the plot. Legend has it that during the shooting of *The Big Sleep* (1946) no one could remember whether a certain character had committed suicide or had been killed (and if so, by whom); so they sent Chandler a telegram, and he couldn't remember, either. The story is absurd, yet plausible: there is a Ponzischeme side to film noir, where long-term logic is routinely sacrificed to immediate effect. And it works: one is never bored, with these films; it's only at the end, when the intrigue collapses like a castle of cards, that you feel a little disappointed—a little betrayed. But after all, betrayal becomes the noir.

The prose of the world. The reduction of others to "means to one's particular ends" returns in a famous section of Hegel's *Aesthetics*:

> The individual man, in order to preserve his individuality, must frequently make himself a means to others, must subserve their limited aims, and must likewise reduce others to mere means in order to satisfy his own interests [. . .] This is the prose of the world [. . .]: a world of finitude and mutability, of entanglement in the relative, of the pressure of necessity from which the individual is in no position to withdraw.*

The prose of the world. "Holly, the world doesn't make any heroes," remarks Welles, wearily, in *The Third Man*; and then, as if suddenly remembering that his friend is a writer of Westerns: "out-

---

* G. W. F. Hegel, *Aesthetics*, cit., p. 149.

side of your stories, of course." *Realpolitik*. The Western needs heroes, because it has no stable mechanism to enforce the law. The hero fills the void of the absent state—he *is* the state. In film noir, the state is perfectly solid, and no one fears for the stability of the social system. There are plenty of transgressions, of course, but they are always local; Stanwyck is dangerous for her husband and a couple of lovers, not for *everybody*. Though occasionally marketed as if they were gangster movies—"Like No Other Picture Since *Scarface* and *Little Caesar*," as the release poster for Kubrick's *The Killing* put it as late as 1956—the atmosphere of the noir is the opposite of 1930s megalomania. Hegel again:

> The prosaic mind treats the vast field of actuality in accordance with [. . .] categories, such as cause and effect, means and end [. . .] literal accuracy, unmistakable definiteness, and clear intelligibility.*

Accuracy and intelligibility: no other genre uses blackboards as happily as film noir. *Bob le Flambeur* (1955) first explains the heist on a large blueprint, and then takes the whole gang to a field where the building is drawn in a 1:1 scale, to make sure they understand the plan ("You have a brain like a pea! How did you get through school?" "I never set foot in one." "I thought so.").† But Hegelian prose is more than just precision, or people "performing certain

---

*G. W. F. Hegel, *Aesthetics*, cit., pp. 974, 1005.
† "Any other questions?" asks Sterling Hayden in *The Killing*. "Good, then let's take a look at this. This is a rough drawing . . . I want you to go over this with me inch by inch . . ." And Sam Jaffe, "the professor," in *The Asphalt Jungle* (1950): "Of course I'll need to do some checking, because the plan is five years old . . . but not much checking [. . .] Everything is here, from the observed routines of the personnel to the alarm system."

definite duties at a certain definite time" (*The Killing*). The synergy of unfettered egoism and intellectual lucidity produces a cynicism all its own. Lifted above the ruins of Vienna in the Prater's giant Ferris wheel, and confronted point-blank about his activity— "Have you ever seen any of your victims?"*—Welles responds by pointing downwards, at the passersby barely visible on the ground below them (Figure 8).

> "Victims? Don't be melodramatic. Look down there . . . Would you feel any pity if one of those . . . dots stopped moving, forever? If I offered you 20,000 pounds for every . . . dot that stopped—would you really, old man, tell me to keep my money? Or would you . . . calculate how many dots you could afford to spare? . . . Free of income tax, old man. Free of income tax."

Dots. "Many people would have fewer qualms at killing a man who was far enough to appear no larger than a swallow, than in butchering an ox with their own hands," Diderot had written in his *Letter on the Blind*.† Physical distance functions as an equivalent for the absence of solidarity—"everything else is nothing to him"—of Hegel's civil society, where everybody is, and remains, *a stranger*. "They swap murders," explains "Bruno" in *Strangers on a Train* (1951): "Each fellow does the other fellow's murder [. . .]

---

* Welles, a black marketer, steals penicillin from hospitals, dilutes it, and sells it for a large profit, causing, among other things, the death of many children. "Kids used to ride this thing a lot in the old days," he observes casually, stepping into the cabin of the wheel, "but they don't have the money now, poor devils."

† On the transformation of this idea from Diderot to *The Genius of Christianity* and *Old Goriot*, see Carlo Ginzburg's "Killing a Chinese Mandarin: The Moral Implications of Distance," *Critical Inquiry* 21, 1994.

Figure 8.

Crisscross." And the assassin of *Murder by Contract*: "The only type of killing that's safe is when a stranger kills a stranger. No motive. Nothing to link the victim to the executioner. Now, why would a stranger kill a stranger? Because somebody's willing to pay. It's business. Same as any other business." And it's a position so icily clear-sighted, the noir never really knows how to respond to it. There are some honest policemen and investigators here, but, despite Chandler's sentimental tirade in "The Simple Art of Murder" (1945)—"Down these mean streets a man must go who is not himself mean, who is neither tarnished nor afraid [. . .] He is the hero, he is everything [. . .] He must be, to use a rather weathered phrase, a man of honor [. . .] He must be the best man in his world and a good enough man for any world . . ."—even the best in film noir lack the ethical halo of the Westerner. They represent *legality*, not legitimacy. And so, when the noir's calculating egoism is finally countered, it is from a very different angle.

Mean what? *Gilda*. Hayworth has been flirting with the clients of her husband's casino, and Ford, who has been charged with keeping an eye on her, wrenches her away from the dance floor:

> "You can't talk to men here like at home. They don't understand it."
>> "Understand what?"
>> "They think you mean it."
>> "Mean what?"
>> "Doesn't it bother you that you're married?"
>> "What I want to know is, does it bother you?"

Like a cartoon therapist, Hayworth repeats every statement in the form of a question: your words mean *so* much more than you want them to. She evokes what Ford has in mind, and lets it hang in the air, unresolved. Shadows. Every time she speaks—from the initial, unforgettable "Me?"—ambiguity takes over. Think of the Western, with its inarticulate men who use their mouth in every possible way—to cough, whistle, spit, yell, chew, chuckle, drink, grimace—except talking; who laugh aloud, but have no idea what irony is. Words don't matter in the Western; in this entire chapter, I have mentioned barely a handful of them. Film noir, is unimaginable without words. Which is to say: without women. Seductive, because they make language seductive. Suggestive, ironic, unstable. "I don't like women," declares the killer of *Murder by Contract*: "they don't stand still." And they don't let men stand still, either. They stimulate desire, *and desire is what finally defeats the* Realpolitik *of prose.* Ethical values couldn't do it; sex can. "What are the two things in life you're most interested in?" the adulterous wife asks her lover in *The Killing*: "Money and women?" What else. The trouble is, that "and" is deceptive: desire interferes with "accuracy and intelligibility," and makes rational conduct impossible: "And then I saw her [. . .] and I knew I wouldn't care about those forty grand." "Excuse me, officer," asks the brain of *The Asphalt Jungle*, who has been captured while watching a girl dance in a bar: "how long have you been out here?" "Two, three minutes . . ." "Ah, yes. About as long as it takes to play a phonograph record." Desire and greed get mixed up, and disrupt all calculations. In *Pushover* (1954), a police entrapment turns quickly into an illicit affair, which Kim Novak is trying to twist into a full murder plan; MacMurray's response—"You win," followed by a long kiss—makes sex and murder one and the same. "You handle [. . .] accident insurance?" asks Stanwyck in the opening gambit of *Double Indemnity*. "Accident insurance? Sure, Mrs. Dietrichson." And in the same breath: "I wish you'd tell me what's engraved on that anklet." Caught. We can already hear the "office memorandum" that opens and closes the film: "Yes, I killed him. I killed him for the money and for a woman. I didn't get the money and I didn't get the woman. Pretty, isn't it?"

III

Hegemony. "In a vast continent of heterogeneous immigrants, coming from all corners of Europe," Perry Anderson has written,

> the products of industrial culture had from the start to be as generic as possible, to maximize their share of the market. In

Europe, every film came out of, and had to play to, cultures with a dense sedimentation of particular traditions, customs, languages inherited from the national past—inevitably generating a cinema with a high local content, with small chance of travelling. In America on the other hand, immigrant publics, with weakened connexions to heteroclite pasts, could only be aggregated by narrative and visual schemas stripped to their most abstract, recursive common denominators. The filmic languages that resolved this problem were, quite logically, those that went on to conquer the world, where the premium on dramatic simplification and repetition, across far more heterogeneous markets, was still greater. The universality of Hollywood forms—US television has never quite been able to repeat their success—derives from this originating task, although like every other dimension of American hegemony, it drew strength from expressly national soil, with the creation of great popular genres drawn from myths of the frontier, the underworld, the Pacific war.*

A hegemony over the world market: Planet Hollywood. And here, the parallel between the Western and film noir—these two mirror images in which every detail is reversed: setting, pace, characters, language, plot—the parallel breaks down, because the impact of the Western on world audiences (and most certainly on European ones) was incomparably greater than that of the other genre. At first this seems strange, given that the noir had been baptized in France, and that so many of its great directors were European (Lang, von Sternberg, Wilder, Siodmak, Curtiz, Preminger, Tourneur, Dassin, Mamoulian, Zinnemann, Maté, Moguy,

---

* Perry Anderson, "Force and Consent," *New Left Review* 17, 2002, pp. 24–25.

Ulmer . . .). But perhaps this is precisely the reason: film noir could be set in Berlin, London, Paris, Vienna; a Frenchman, Jean-Pierre Melville, would soon emerge as its greatest stylist. By contrast, the Western was profoundly American, and that's what postwar European audiences wanted, in film just as in music, drinks, clothes, dancing, and other fields of everyday life. A new start. Plus, its balance of hope and realism was perfect for post-1945 Europe: the hope of a space so incommensurably larger than that of continental nation-states, it seemed to offer room for (almost) everybody; and the realism of films that didn't avert their eyes from the spectacle of violence (which, for a generation that had lived through the war, would have been absurd) yet invented a hero—a mix of old and new: a knight with a gun—capable of keeping it under control. Much more than war films, Westerns were the great postwar form, not just in a chronological, but in a symbolic sense; films for which violence and death constituted the great problem—the "dissonance," in Lukács's metaphor—that asked for an aesthetic resolution. The Western, of course, was not "caused" by the war: it had been in existence, first in literature and then in film, for almost a century. But the war offered it the opportunity to activate all its symbolic potential. As one generation (and one war) earlier with Hemingway, a mostly European trauma found an answer in an American form; but this time, instead of a cautious recovery from the ferocity of history, violence was incorporated into the story, becoming one of its indispensable ingredients. And with this, American cultural hegemony began in earnest.

CAUSALITY IN *DEATH OF A SALESMAN*

American tragedy. American myths, everywhere. A nuclear family, their home—and their mortgage. "I made the last payment on the house today," murmurs Linda in her final speech, in front of Willy's grave. "We're free and clear [. . .] We are free . . . We are free . . ."* Free: the supreme American value—displaced, typically, from politics to the economy—is the last word of the play; and *only* its last word, never once uttered before Willy's burial. There is the pioneer-like theme of "doing things with one's hands"; but Willy's gardening, always irrelevant, has turned by the end of the evening into a painful folly. There is salesmanship: the jovial embellishment of commodities for the purpose of profit, that somehow no longer seems to work. There is sports, as a more manly form of social mobility than the school Willy despises, and the typically American dream that the next generation will have

---

*Arthur Miller, *Death of a Salesman*, 1949, Penguin, Harmondsworth, 1976, p. 139.

a better life than their parents: two hopes bluntly brought to nothing by Biff's bitter failure. There is the car: which at first brings prosperity ("Chevrolet, Linda, is the greatest car ever built" [34]), and ultimately death. American myths, everywhere: and they all turn to ashes.

Attention must be paid.   Let's begin with a moment that stands at an odd angle to the rest of the play. Linda and her sons are having a harsh confrontation about Willy, and Biff is being particularly unforgiving: "Stop making excuses for him! [. . .] He never had an ounce of respect for you [. . .] Charley wouldn't do this." At this point, Linda reacts:

> Then make Charley your father, Biff. You can't do that, can you? I don't say he's a great man. Willy Loman never made a lot of money. His name was never in the paper. He's not the finest character that ever lived. But he's a human being, and a terrible thing is happening to him. So attention must be paid. He's not to be allowed to fall into his grave like an old dog. Attention, attention must be finally paid to such a person. You called him crazy . . . [56]

Attention must be paid. Strange way of saying things. Must be paid . . . by whom? By Biff and Happy, clearly enough, who are standing right there, in front of their mother. But by having Linda address an unspecified listener, Miller makes her words transcend that particular moment in the plot, and address the audience as a whole; possibly, an even larger audience than that which is present in the theater. Willy's fate should concern, not only his family, but all of society. That's where the awkward mix of the imperative ("must . . .) and the passive (. . . be paid") comes from: it's an echo of those formulations ("tickets must be validated," "engines must be turned off") which public authorities—and the theater, at its best, *has* been a public authority—adopt in their injunctions. This larger horizon also explains the shift from the second person typical of dramatic dialogue—perfectly visible near the margins of the passage: "Then make Charley *your* father, Biff. *You* can't do that, can *you*? [. . .] *You* called him crazy . . ."—to the third person, so unusual in plays: "I don't say *he's* a great man . . . *his* name . . . *he's* not . . . *he's* . . . *him* . . . *he's* . . . *his.*" All these choices create a distance between the audience and the scene, making it sound—strange. It's the *ostranenje* ("estrangement") of Russian Formalism: an aesthetic strategy that, by presenting reality in an unexpected way ("defamiliarization" is another standard English translation of the term), makes us see it "as if for the first time."* And strange also in the sense of Brecht's *Verfremdungseffekt* (estrangement effect), where Formalist "surprise" joins forces with Marx's "alienation" (another meaning of *Verfremdung*), thus presenting reality as both unfamiliar *and wrong.*† Unfamiliar: Linda's words place Willy's situation in a new light, prompting Biff's "I didn't mean . . ." and Happy's "I didn't know . . ." Wrong: a man is being treated like a dying dog, and something has to be done. "Finally," adds Linda.‡ Not only should we pay attention to people like Willy;

---

* See Viktor Shklovsky, "Art as Device," 1917, later collected in *Theory of Prose*, 1929, Dalkey Archive Press, 1990, *passim.*

† "The production took the subject-matter and the incidents shown, and put them through a process of alienation: the alienation that is necessary to all understanding." Bertolt Brecht, "Theatre for Pleasure or Theatre for Instruction," cit., p. 71.

‡ Linda's line is usually delivered as "attention must finally be paid to such a person," making the "finally" sink into near-invisibility, as adverbs routinely do. Miller's actual word sequence, however—"Attention *must be finally paid* to

we should have started doing so a long time ago. This has gone on for too long, and there is almost no time left. Almost; it's still only the first act of the play, Biff has just come home, has an idea, something may happen, perhaps as early as tomorrow . . .

White collar. Attention must be paid . . . to whom? Not "to your father," or "to my husband," but: "to such a person." After the generalization of the audience—attention must be paid *by everybody*—comes that of the object: it must be paid *to all people like Willy Loman.* A social class. Salesmen. Two years after Miller's play, Wright Mills's *White Collar: The American Middle Classes*—a study of Macy's employees in New York: the temple of American salesmanship—provided a memorable portrait of this social group. "In the world of the small entrepreneur," Mills wrote, "selling was one activity among many, limited in scope, technique, and manner [. . .] In the new society," however,

> selling is a pervasive activity, unlimited in scope and ruthless in its choice of technique and manner [. . .] Salesmanship is much too important to be left to pep alone or to the personal flair of detached salesmen [. . .] In selling, as elsewhere, centralization has meant the expropriation of certain traits previously found in creative salesmen.*

"In those days there was personality in it," mourns Willy, recalling a salesman he had encountered in his youth:

---

such a person"—by (mis)placing the adverb in a slightly ungrammatical position, forces us to—finally—hear it "as if for the first time."

*C. Wright Mills, *White Collar: The American Middle Classes*, 1951, Oxford UP, 2002, pp. 161, 178–79.

There was respect, and comradeship, and gratitude in it. Today,
it's all cut and dried, and there's no chance for bringing friendship to bear—or personality. You see what I mean? [81]

"Friendship" is too strong a word for what Willy is talking about,
but it points in the right direction: towards that "personally known
market" (Mills again), where the salesman's key relationship was
"not with their superior or bosses, but with the customers." That
too, however, is now a thing of the past: in the "new society" in
which Willy has to work, customers have turned into a hostile
multitude—"They seem to laugh at me [. . .] they just pass me by"—
while the encounter with his boss, Howard Wagner, occupies the
center of the plot. It's the "tomorrow" evoked in the previous paragraph: the beginning of the second act of the play. Biff has left
early, to find financial backing for his sporting goods idea, and
will meet his father for dinner. "It's changing. Willy, I can feel it
changing!" exclaims Linda at breakfast [74]. "Beyond a question,"
replies Willy. And off he goes.

The capital of Alabama. As Willy walks into his office [76–84],
Howard Wagner is playing with the tape recorder he has bought
the day before; and Willy, who has no idea what the gadget is for,
looks immediately out of step with the times. He asks Howard four
times if they can talk, and is either ignored, or rebuked for being
a nuisance. Voices emerge from the recorder and take over the
stage: Howard's daughter, whistling a tune; his five-year-old son
("The capital of Alabama is Montgomery"); his wife ("I can't think
of anything"). It could be the turning point of the play: it is
crammed with babble. Then, when Willy finally manages to get
Howard's attention, it quickly becomes clear that he has nothing

to offer, and nothing to claim; after a weak replica of Linda's "not be allowed to fall into his grave like an old dog" ("You can't eat the orange and throw the peel away—a man is not a piece of fruit!"), Willy slides into the past ("Remember, Christmas time— when you had the party here?"), sinking further and further back ("Your father came to me the day you were born [. . .] When I was a boy—eighteen, nineteen [. . .] In 1928 I had a big year . . ."), and ending with the wistful recollection of an eighty-four-year-old salesman working from the comfort of a hotel room in his "green velvet slippers" ("And when I saw that, I realized that selling was the greatest career a man could want").* In a crescendo of humiliation, Howard turns away from Willy, addresses him as "kid," and then fires him. But even more striking than this turn of events is the uncanny *absence of pathos* that characterizes the scene. It has been the decisive encounter of Willy's life—the death sentence of the traveling salesman, as it were—but it certainly doesn't feel like it. The language sounds wrong. "The completely dramatic form is the *dialogue*," writes Hegel in his analysis of tragic form in the *Aesthetics*:

> for in it alone can the individual agents express face to face their character and aim [. . .] their animating "pathos" [. . .] the ethically justified "pathos" which they assert against one another with eloquence not in sentimental and personal rhetoric or in the

---

* It is at this point, incidentally, that the expression "death of a salesman" occurs in the play, in the sense of "the kind of death every salesman would like to have": on the train between New York and Boston, getting ready for work. The indefinite article in the play's title has, however, the opposite implication: not the best end a salesman could hope for, but the death of a salesman *like anybody else*—a salesman without qualities.

sophistries of passion, but in solid and cultivated objective language.*

This is what is missing here. To speak of "eloquence" for Howard's "'Cause you gotta admit, business is business," and "Look, kid, I'm busy this morning," would be absurd. And as for Willy, his pathos is not agonistic but elegiac ("When he died, hundreds of salesmen and buyers were at his funeral . . ."). The two registers alternate without connecting, let alone confronting each other. But why? It's the turning point of the plot—why is language so unable to express it?

Gegeneinander. On this, the best answer was given by Brecht in an essay from the 1930s, where he observed that, in the aftermath of World War I, it had become clear that "the most important transactions between people could no longer be shown simply by personifying the motive forces."† In terms of *Death of a Salesman*: if the "motive forces" of the plot are the structural transformations of salesmanship diagnosed in *White Collar*, then Willy's fate is decided at a level where his words and Howard's are completely irrelevant, and it makes sense that their face-to-face—the *"gegeneinander"* ("one-against-the-other"), which was for Hegel the cornerstone of dramatic collision—should lack the "ethically justified pathos" of the *Aesthetics*, and the scene be taken over by Howard's silly fixation with the tape recorder, or Willy's sentimentalization of the past. Say whatever you like, the play seems to suggest—it really doesn't matter anymore: the death sentence is coming from impersonal forces that work behind the scenes and

---

*G. W. F. Hegel, *Aesthetics*, cit., pp. 1172–73, 1214–55.
†Bertolt Brecht, "Theatre for Pleasure or Theatre for Instruction," cit., p. 70.

don't care for the concrete words of concrete individuals. The trouble is, the concrete words of concrete individuals are (almost) all a play has at its disposal. If they no longer matter, how can the theater survive?

As the car speeds off. Let's leave this question open for now, and in fact add to it a second one: Why *death* of a salesman? The salesman dies, yes, but so do many dramatic characters, without their death being announced before the play even begins. Another text with a similar title—Georg Büchner's *Danton's Death* (1835), which covers Danton's last few days before being sent to the guillotine—sheds some light on the question. Peter Szondi:

> Unlike Phaedra, Hamlet and Demetrius, whose deaths do not
> need to be mentioned in the title, Danton is characterized less
> by the fact that he must die and more by the fact that he cannot
> die, for he is already dead.*

A death that has already occurred, and of which we witness only the prolonged agony. In Danton's case, the cause is the French Revolution itself: he is "already dead" in the sense that his "political moment" (Lukács) has passed, and will never return; all he can do is survive, with less and less conviction. And the same for Willy: his "historical moment"—the time when a traveling salesman could bring middle-class comfort to his family—is gone, and he moves spectrally around, bouncing from one interaction to the next, without sense of direction or purpose. Except for one moment: his suicide. When "the car speeds off, [and] the music crashes down in a frenzy of sound"—great touch, having man and car be

---

*Peter Szondi, *An Essay on the Tragic*, 1961, Stanford UP, 2002, p. 100.

united in life and in death, like a knight and his horse—Willy appears to regain mastery over his own fate. "Appears to": because what really happens, in that handful of seconds, is in fact far from obvious. Though a suicide is the likeliest explanation,* an accident remains also possible,† and a definite answer is therefore impossible—as it is, incidentally, for Büchner's *Danton*, and many other modern plays.‡ This uncertainty between suicide and accident marks a fundamental difference between modern drama and ancient and Renaissance tragedy, and I cannot discuss it in detail here; but I want to make clear that speaking of an "accident" is not meant to suggest that Willy's death is a purely random event. Even if it *were* accidental, his death would be the result of

---

* In the first act, Linda mentions the piece of tubing she has found behind the gas furnace; in the second, Willy talks about his life insurance with Charley, and, immediately before his death, with Ben; at some point, Linda also tells Biff and Happy of a witness who is convinced that one of Willy's "accidents" was in fact a deliberate attempt to drive the car off a bridge.

† Willy has never tried to use the piece of tubing behind the furnace, nor has he noticed its disappearance; and in the final scene he may be driving away in despair, or in a state of hallucination: after all, his last few sentences before dying are addressed, first to his dead brother, Ben, and then to Biff as a teenager. Furthermore, the possibility of an accident had been evoked in the very first scene of the play, when Willy tells Linda of having absentmindedly almost driven off the road.

‡ Danton's inaction is seen by some characters as a form of indirect suicide—while for others it is just a sign of his being completely out of touch with reality. Ibsen, who is arguably the strongest influence on Miller's dramaturgy, is another significant case in point. In *The Master Builder*, suicide and vertigo are equally likely as causes of Solness's death, while in *The Wild Duck*—though it is quite probable that Hedvig means to kill herself—the girl may also be trying on her own body the position from which to shoot the duck, whose sacrifice has been the topic of her long and ambiguous conversation with Gregers. ("The wild duck" are the last words she utters, immediately before disappearing into the attic.) Similar arguments can be made for *Hedda Gabler, John Gabriel Borkman*, and *When We Dead Awaken*.

the physical and mental collapse caused by his working conditions: it would have a "cause." The problem is, this cause would lack the sense of *necessity* we expect from drama: Willy's interminable drives may have made his death *more likely to happen*, but hardly inevitable. In a novel, this element of "probability" would be perfectly appropriate; in drama, it's a sign of what Bakhtin has called the "novelization" of modern literature: the conventions and worldview of the novel infiltrating other genres, and reshaping them in depth. But can drama let itself be reshaped by novelistic conventions—having its protagonist die in an accident—without losing its *raison d'être*?

Miller vs. Miller. Let's try to weave together these various threads. Two major episodes of *Death of a Salesman*—Willy's layoff and his possibly "accidental" death—are both caused by "motive forces" (the transformations of postwar salesmanship, and the ensuing working conditions) that cannot be represented in dramatic form, and that therefore bring into the text a large dose of uncertainty (how exactly does Willy die), or pure and simple noise (all the random quirks around his layoff). The historical intelligence of American society seems to be at odds with the structural constraints of the theater, and the way Miller addresses the contrast becomes a clue of what he considers essential to the play's project. The desultory pace of the layoff scene, for instance, doesn't seem to bother him: its lack of focus may weaken the political dimension of *Death of a Salesman*, but that's not enough to prompt a major intervention. Willy's death is already a different story: though the possibility of an accident is a *Leitmotiv* of the play from its very first scene, it is then increasingly confined to the background, whereas allusions to suicide move to the foreground of the dialogue. It's as if Miller were aware of the two conflicting possibilities, and wanted to restore the centrality of dramatic conventions by having Willy kill himself—like Ajax, Antigone, Othello, Phèdre—rather than succumb to the pressure of circumstances like so many novelistic characters. But the most revealing instance of Miller working against the logic of his own creation is an episode I haven't yet mentioned, though every time I pick up my Penguin edition of the play I cannot but notice that it occupies the cover of the book. I haven't mentioned it, because *Death of a Salesman* doesn't really need it; Penguin put it on the cover, because it's arguably the most memorable moment of the entire evening. Odd.

Boston. *Death of a Salesman* is the story of a triple failure: of Willy as a salesman, of Willy's dreams about Biff, and of Biff as an athlete. "I never got anywhere because you blew me so full of hot air I could never stand taking orders from anybody!" he shouts to his father in the confrontation near the end of the second act, and his words—corroborated by the play's frequent flashbacks—are a perfect explanation for his failure. Willy has always, not just condoned, but encouraged Biff's bullying and prevarication, and it's easy to imagine how this story could unfold: Biff in college, expelled for cheating on his exams; his coach benching him for his conceited arrogance; or he could turn out to be a mediocre player after all, as is the case with most high school stars, or have one of those frequent, banal career-ending injuries. There are so many ways for dreams—American or otherwise—to be undone by the friction of ordinary circumstances: Willy himself has suffered this fate, and there would be nothing more plausible—nor, in its way, more powerful—than duplicating his destiny in that of his older son. But how can drama show that "pleasureless yielding to the small solicitations of circumstance which is a commoner history of perdition than any single momentous bargain"? *Middlemarch* is a novel, and even there it's not easy. In drama? It's the same bifurcation, one more time: historical understanding *versus* dramatic conventions. And this time, Miller makes a very different choice. Biff's high school friend Bernard is telling Willy about the moment when Biff's life changed once and for all:

> BERNARD: [. . .] I got the idea that he'd gone up to New England to see you. Did he have a talk with you then? *(Willy stares in silence.)*
>
> BERNARD: Willy?
>
> WILLY *(with a strong edge of resentment in his voice)*: Yeah, he came to Boston. What about it?
>
> BERNARD: Well, just that when he came back—I'll never forget this, [he] took his sneakers—remember those sneakers with "University of Virginia" printed on them? He was so proud of those, wore them every day. And he took them down in the cellar, and burned them up in the furnace [. . .] I've often thought of how strange it was that I knew he'd given up his life. What happened in Boston, Willy? [94]

What happened was this: that Biff showed up unexpectedly at Willy's hotel, and found him with a woman. Placed just before the end, without any preparation, and clearly meant as an answer to Bernard's question, Boston completely changes our sense of the plot, and of the plague that haunts the Loman family. If Biff went wrong, and Willy went wrong, and everything went wrong, it's because Biff discovered Willy's affair. Forget salesmanship and working conditions, the myth of sports and the secret delight in intimidation: Boston makes all structural explanations superfluous. Out of sexual moralism? Always possible; but since the play contains no other hint in this direction, I doubt it. If the scene was so important for Miller, it wasn't for "ethical" reasons, but because it restored that "personification of the motive forces" that Brecht had declared no longer plausible; it returned *Death of a Salesman* to a world of concrete individual actions—it returned it *to the theater, and at its most theatrical*: in the Boston episode, stage directions become all-important: Biff knocks "off left," the Woman "vanishes into the wing," the light moves towards Biff, the Woman re-enters . . . It could be a nineteenth-century farce. It's the cheapest, most melodramatic moment of the entire evening; but it's also unforgettable, because, for once, all that matters is what happens in front of our eyes. It's a pity that, in looking at it, we forget the true intelligence of *Death of a Salesman*.

AMSTERDAM, NEW AMSTERDAM

I

The storyteller. Of the forty or so paintings by Jan Vermeer, more than half represent scenes like the one in Figure 9. *Girl Interrupted at Her Music* (c. 1658–69) is the title by which it usually goes; but perhaps it's not so simple. With the instrument abandoned on the table and covered by the score, it's unlikely that the girl *was* making music at the moment she was interrupted; nor is it clear what she and her teacher (*is* he a teacher?) are looking at; for sure, it looks different from the score on the table. And what exactly is the "interruption" about? Why is the girl turning, while the "teacher" is not? How close their hands are, fingers almost bound to touch under the paper they are holding; he, enveloping her in a gesture that has no equivalent in the male figure of the other *Music Lesson* (1662–63)—nor in any of Vermeer's male figures, for that matter. And the expression on the girl's face: neither surprised nor worried; slightly ironic, perhaps? Slightly

Figure 9.

haughty? The painting offers no answer to these questions; all it gives us is this politely enigmatic scene from a story we will never know. And that other girl, in *Officer and Smiling Girl* (1658): so innocent, almost childlike in the trusting openness of her smile. But what stories has he been telling her, one wonders, to capture her attention, the glass of wine half forgotten between her hands? And who *is* he? (What an idea, placing those broad shoulders, those showy garments, right in front of our eyes—and then hiding his face.) *Mistress and Maid* (1667–68): the maid hands her mistress a letter, interrupting the writing of *another* letter; how many epistolary novels are going on, in this bourgeois household? *Lady Writing a Letter with Her Maid* (1670): the maid, looking towards the window; is someone waiting for an answer out there? Is *the maid* expecting someone? Or is she acting as a sentinel, making sure her mistress is not surprised at the writing table? And so on, and on, until the real question becomes not "Is the maid acting as a sentinel?" but rather: Why all these little mysteries in Vermeer's work?

Girl asleep, woman reading a letter. A possible answer lies in Roland Barthes's subdivision of narrative episodes into "nuclei"— major turning points that change the general direction of the story—and "catalysts," or "fillers," that keep the plot moving from one turning point to the next, without altering its fundamental trajectory.* The small mysteries of Vermeer's paintings are exactly what fillers are made of: a lady is writing a letter, and maybe she is even writing to a secret lover; but there is no sign that it is her *first* letter (or her last, for that matter); it is *one* episode in her novel, not the decisive one. A girl is smiling to a somewhat alarming officer; for the moment, she is *just* smiling. The situation is open, without being dramatic. Tellingly, the X-ray of Vermeer's first "narrative" painting—the *Girl Asleep* of 1657, now at the Metropolitan Museum—revealed a shift from one type of episode to the other: initially, the scene included a man moving in the room in the background, with a strong suggestion of threat, given how vulnerable the sleeping girl seems to be. But then Vermeer erased the looming figure, left the second room empty, and never returned

* See Roland Barthes, "Introduction to the Structural Analysis of Narratives," 1966, in Susan Sontag, ed., *Barthes: Selected Writings*, Hill and Wang, New York, 1982, especially pp. 265–66.

Figure 10.

to that kind of composition again. His is a *safe* world, which allows everyday existence to levitate into open-endedness, while keeping it firmly within the limits of bourgeois sociability: making music, writing, reading, conversing, courting . . . A lively, yet composed rehearsal of one's position within a social class and its culture: this is what happens in these domestic "narratives." It's a world with such a confident sense of belonging, it emanates even from a solitary figure like the *Woman in Blue* (1662–64) of the Rijksmuseum: so absorbed in the letter she is reading, we feel the presence of a powerful relationship—of a "society"—even though no one else

Figure 11.

is visible on the canvas. People are often on their own, in Vermeer; lonely, never.

Automat. Edward Hopper's world is at once a distant echo of Vermeer's, and its point-by-point reversal. In his twentieth-century America, the bright everyday of early modern Holland returns to the old connotations of the term: the everyday as a colorless succession of blank, uneventful days. The man in *Sunday* (1926; Figure 10) is alone, not in the sense that no one else is with him, but because he doesn't seem to *expect* anyone anymore. There he sits, small, crouched, staring into the void. *Automat* (1927; Figure 11): a kind of restaurant where people collected their food directly from machines, making human contact unnecessary; and a woman, alone, in an empty room where even the heater seems to add to the cold. And the titles of these paintings: spaces, times (*Automat, Sunday, Office in a Small Town, Early Sunday Morning, Room in New York, Morning in a City* . . .)—but no hint of activity. Vermeer's people were always *doing* something: if they weren't usually working in the proper sense of the word (though there is *Maid Pouring Milk*, in 1660, and the *Lacemaker* of 1669–70), they were reading, writing, listening, playing the lute, trying on a necklace. Active. Hopper's figures, even when nominally at work (*Office in a Small Town*, 1953), are so stiff, they seem to have been hypnotized. Not action, but its *suspension* is his great theme: *Nighthawks* (1942): so late at night, nothing can happen anymore; a "filler," filled with nothing. The woman of *Automat* is touching the handle of the cup; will she ever drink? (Or has she already, and is now postponing the moment of leaving?) *Chop Suey* (1928): two women across a small table, looking past each other's face; empty bowls, a teapot without cups. *Room in New York* (1932; Figure 12): a man reading a paper, a woman twisted uncomfortably away from him. There is an episode in *Madame Bovary*—"a fragment that contains the entire story," as Auerbach put it in *Mimesis*—in which Emma's loneliness, as she waits for her lethargic husband to finish his dinner, is condensed in her "entertaining herself [. . .] drawing lines over the oilcloth with the point of her knife." The same here: though next to the piano, the woman is definitely not playing; she's just killing time, one finger sliding aimlessly over the keys, waiting for the man to finish reading. And then, what? She seems to have dressed up for the evening; he seems not to have noticed. There is definitely a story behind this scene, but *only* behind it; in the future, nothing.

Figure 12.

Figure 13.

Room and window. The depth of Vermeer: the two women of *The Love Letter* (1669–70; Figure 13), placed quite far from us, in the middle of the back room, with a laundry basket in front of them; and then clogs, a mop, a doorframe, shelves with papers and other objects . . . The figures in *Girl Interrupted at Her Music*, *Girl with a Wineglass* (1659–60), and *Lady Standing at the Virginal* (1673–75) are turned towards the viewer in such a way that the space between them and us becomes part of the painting; we are the ones who have interrupted the music lesson, and entered the room. Even when the scene is close to the picture plane, as in *Officer and Smiling Girl*, a multiplicity of spatial strata—the officer's chair; the sitting man; the table; the girl; her chair; the wall behind her—accentuate the depth of what looks like a very small room. It's a conception of domestic space that must have arisen from the architecture of early modern Dutch cities, with their narrow houses developing "inwards," in depth, like cake slices, away from the public world of street and canal; a disposition that must have intensified the sense of the private sphere (and which in Vermeer always ends in a wall, as if to indicate the existence of a "private within the private"—the bedroom—which remains off limits to representation). Then one returns to *Room in New York*, and realizes that the axis has rotated 90 degrees: what used to be deep is now horizontal and flat. There is still an "inside," here, but it's no longer an "interior": though the piano suggests a private apartment, the whole feels more like a hotel: anodyne paintings, yellowish wallpaper, an empty table—a total absence of individual touches. The space is cramped, uncomfortable; the sill of the large open window intruding into the room, as if placing it under siege. "Wall apertures," Le Corbusier called the new horizontal windows of twentieth-century architecture, hailing them as the protagonists of a new domestic space in which they would allow "light

Figure 14.

and air to enter copiously."* Light and air, in the painter of electricity and enclosed spaces? This is not the function of such an oversize window, but rather: laying bare the private sphere, depriving it of any protection against public scrutiny; making it not just visible, but *inspectable* from the outside. Society, as a giant aquarium.

Nothing, it seemed, could be done. A lifeless private sphere; and deserted public spaces. *Drug Store* (1927; Figure 14): closed. *Early Sunday Morning* (1930): empty. It's Sunday morning, and early, so

* The expression appears in the manifesto "Five Points Towards a New Architecture," written by Le Corbusier and Pierre Jeanneret in 1926; now in Ulrich Conrads, ed., *Programs and Manifestos on 20th-Century Architecture*, MIT Press, 1971, p. 100. My thanks to Daniel Jütte for having made me aware of Le Corbusier's ideas about windows.

Figure 15.

it makes sense that no one is around. But in art, causality is always teleology in disguise: no one had forced Hopper to paint a pharmacy after hours, or a street on Sunday; if he did so, it's because it allowed him to present an emptiness so radical, it contradicted the very idea of the public. Public, *populus*, people; but not here. It's the achievement of *Nighthawks* (Figure 15): fitting four people in a small space, and making it look empty just the same. And it *is* an achievement, deliberately pursued, sketch after sketch, by intensifying all signs of overall disconnection. "As the studies progress the windows become larger and larger," Judith Barter has observed, whereas the human figures "become smaller, and are pushed to the right."* The man and woman at the bar were initially closer to each other; in one version, they seem to be touching; in another, he appears to be talking to her. One small step at a time—the barman more insulated from the rest, the left corner stretched

---

*Judith A. Barter, *"Nighthawks*: Transcending Reality," in Barter et al., *Edward Hopper*, Thames and Hudson, London, 2007, p. 200.

farther away, the couple pulled apart, the ceiling made higher, the street broader, the buildings taller—Hopper emptied out his own canvas. There they are: four people alone at night, postponing their return to a "room in New York." And after all, returning to what? I have said that Hopper's people are inactive, and they certainly are; but *unemployed* would be more to the point. Though his first major paintings precede the Great Depression by a few years, it's the mood of the 1930s that has turned them into powerful symbols of American life. "Everyone suffered from a sense of utter hopelessness," wrote John Kenneth Galbraith of those years: "nothing, it seemed, could be done. And given the ideas which controlled policy, nothing could be done."* Whence the ominous quality of Hopper's mornings: far from conveying the feeling of a new beginning—Vermeer's sunlight, streaming warmly through his small windows—they make action appear utterly unimaginable. *Morning in a City* (1944): a woman, standing, looking out the window, naked and motionless in a barren room. There is something *Endgame*-like in her pose; a distant, nebulous memory of other human beings out there. But a spell holds her captive, like everybody else in these paintings: *Cape Cod Morning* (1950), *Morning Sun* (1952), *South Carolina Morning* (1955): everybody looking out, and no one *venturing* out. Wax figures, in anemic light.

II

Time passes. Why is it that "what we call 'the soul' expresses itself in the clearest fashion" in the human face, asked Georg

---

*John Kenneth Galbraith, *The Great Crash: 1929*, 1954, Houghton Mifflin, Boston, 1961, p. 192.

Simmel in 1901, posing what is clearly *the* question for any theory of the portrait? That the face is usually bare and exposed, while the body is covered—hence potentially "hidden"—is certainly part of the answer. But Simmel goes further:

> We may consider the act of turning the multiplicity of worldly ele-
> ments into a unity as the most typical activity of the spirit [. . .]
> The more tightly the inter-connected parts respond to each
> other, the more their disunion turns into a lively interaction,
> the more pervaded by a spiritual unity the whole appears [. . .]
> Within the human body, the face is the highest instance of such
> unity.*

No single facial feature, no matter how striking—eyes, mouth, nose, jaw—holds the secret of expression; it's only the capacity to *unify* them that expresses "the activity of the spirit," making us think of "the soul." And the greatest example of this, for Simmel, is Rembrandt's forty-year-long series of eighty-eight self-portraits, which stretched from the beginning of his adult life to the time of his death. At the beginning of the cycle, individual features still stand out as such, almost detaching themselves from the rest of the face: the mouth, nose, and right eye in *Self-Portrait with Gorget* (c. 1629); the hair in *Self-Portrait as a Young Man* (1629); the cheek and lips in *Self-Portrait with Gorget and Beret* (c. 1629; Figure 16). With the passage of time, though, the prominence of these isolated traits ebbs slowly away: the lips that seemed on the verge of say-ing a few sharp words lose their tension, and come to rest quietly one on top of the other; the eyes no longer challenge the world,

---

*Georg Simmel, "Die ästhetische Bedeutung des Gesichts," *Der Lotse. Ham-burgische Wochenschrift für deutsche Kultur*, June 1901, p. 280.

Figure 16.

and in fact no longer even seem to look out "into" the world; they absorb what is around them with an attitude of patient acceptance. The neck thickens, and retracts between the shoulders; the face descends into the body; it *becomes* body. The self-portraits present "the continuity of the flowing totality of life," wrote Simmel in his study of Rembrandt;[*] and the flow is a deep, irreversible process of *amalgamation*. Take the color that dominates the early portraits; the color of youth: white. Eyes, teeth, cheeks, neck; a body—and a soul?—that has not yet been touched by life.[†] Then,

---

[*] Georg Simmel, *Rembrandt: An Essay in the Philosophy of Art*, 1916, Routledge, London, 2005, p. 11.

[†] Vermeer's whites are of course even more unsullied—one might say: virginal—than Rembrandt's. *Officer and Smiling Girl*: the girl's collar, headdress,

Figure 17.

as Rembrandt ages, the white converts gradually into a pasty gray-brown, while the opposition between light and shadow—that had divided the face into two along the ridge of the nose in *Self-Portrait with Gorget*, or created a mysterious halo around the cheek in *Self-Portrait with Gorget and Beret*—starts to lose its clarity; eventually, in the Vienna *Self-Portrait* (c. 1657; Figure 17), or the Edinburgh *Self-Portrait with Beret and Turned-up Collar* (1659), light and darkness are no longer in antithesis to each other. Amalgamation,

---

forehead; the map and the wall behind her; and especially all those minute details that make her visage so incredibly luminous: the strokes of white on her incisors, lower lip, chin, nose . . . The same in *Girl with the Pearl Earring* (1665): the pearl, the collar, the whites of her eyes—even two tiny specks of white in her pupils!

Figure 18.

everywhere; and as its substratum, the humblest of all facial features: the skin. Extending around the mouth and eyes, over nose and forehead and cheeks, the skin of the ageing Rembrandt absorbs the extraordinary mix of hues—yellow, green, gray, purple, black—of the Washington *Self-Portrait with Beret and Turned-up Collar* (1659; Figure 18). If there is a color of time, this must be it: it shows the scars and wrinkles, the swellings and burns and blemishes that the world has traced over Rembrandt's body, eroding the separation between inside and outside. Entropy: this is the great law behind the eighty-eight visages. Slow, irrevocable loss of distinction. "Time passes": the middle section of *To the Lighthouse*, which describes the slow-motion collapse of a once-elegant house:

The long night seemed to have set in; the trifling airs, nibbling, the clammy breaths, fumbling, seemed to have triumphed. The saucepan had rusted and the mat decayed. Toads had nosed their way in. Idly, aimlessly, the swaying shawl swung to and fro [. . .] the floor was strewn with straw; the plaster fell in shovelfuls; rafters were laid bare . . .*

Rusted and decayed: Rembrandt's bruised skin and subdued eyes. As he approaches the final part of his life, writes Simmel,

it is as if death were the steady further development of this flowing totality of life—like the current with which it flows into the sea, and not through violation by some other factor, but only following its natural course from the beginning. [74]

Death as a current that mingles its waters with those of the sea. Let's remember this image.

Assembly line. Before becoming one of the most famous portraitists of the late twentieth century, Andy Warhol seemed headed in a very different direction. His first solo show consisted of thirty-two identical paintings of white, red, gold, and black cans, whose only recognizable difference consisted in the type of soup indicated on the label (*Campbell's Soup Cans*, 1962; Figure 19). The MoMA, where the paintings now are, has neatly arranged them in four tight rows of eight canvases each, as if they were a giant page of postage stamps; but Warhol's initial idea had been quite different— or more precisely, it hadn't been an idea at all: when he sent them to the Ferus Gallery, in Los Angeles, in the summer of 1962, the

* Virginia Woolf, *To the Lighthouse*, 1927, HBJ, London, 1989, p. 137.

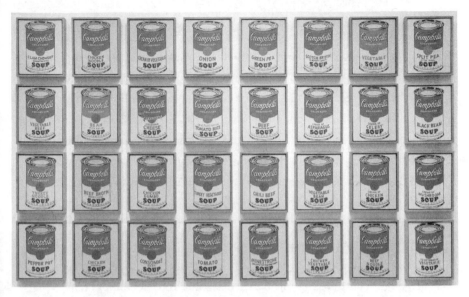

Figure 19.

canvases "were not conceived as a single work of art. They were meant to be *shown* together, but then sold separately."* It was the gallerist, Irving Blum, who changed everything, by making two decisions that shaped the public perception of Warhol for decades to come. First, he hung the canvases in a single long row, making them rest on a narrow ledge that evoked a supermarket shelf: a choice that framed the paintings as industrial commodities, and triggered a flurry of comments on the surrender of art to the market.† But then, instead of letting the art market dismember

---

* Kirk Varnedoe, *"Campbell's Soup Cans, 1962,"* in Heiner Bastian, ed., *Warhol: A Retrospective*, Tate Publishing, London, 2001, p. 41.

† Given that *Campbell's Soup Cans* drew attention to the labels of the cans, which had (also) the function of attracting the gaze of potential buyers, the work bound together art, advertising, and the industrial production of commodities, as if suggesting that they may have something important in common. And indeed, just as modern art is placed by definition beyond truth

Campbell's Soup Cans as it pleased, Blum bought back the five canvases that had already been sold—for a hundred dollars apiece, one of them to the actor Dennis Hopper—because he had become convinced that the thirty-two paintings should remain together. (Warhol agreed, and sold him the entire set for a thousand dollars.) Thanks to Blum, then, *Campbell's Soup Cans* was effectively redefined as a single work articulated into a series of images. Series: that's the key. It's a notion that was already *in nuce* in the catalogues of *Leaves of Grass*, which had projected over American space a magic equilbrium between the *pluribus* of semantic contents (that kept changing from one "free" verse to the next) and the *unum* of grammar (that stamped the same basic structures everywhere). Variety and sameness were both present then, and both equally strong; a century later, the balance is gone, and the point of *Campbell's Soup Cans* lies in showing how incredibly *uniform* things have become in the age of mechanical reproduction. And Warhol relished the uniformity:* that's why he called his New York studio

---

and falsehood, advertising is (usually) neither exactly truthful nor exactly deceitful, and—to turn to the literal "content" of the cans themselves—canned soup is itself neither completely natural nor completely artificial. It is the overlap of these three "neither-nors" that makes *Campbell's Soup Cans* so equivocally compelling.

*On this point, the contrast with Hopper is striking. Hopper, too, had been aware of the uniformity of modern production (in his case, urban architecture): one need only think of the ten identical windows of *Early Sunday Morning*, let alone the hundred and fifty of *Apartment Houses, East River* (1930). But his paintings concentrate on the *difference* that continues to exist within the series: some windows of *Early Sunday Morning* are open and others are closed, curtains are unevenly raised, there are patches of white, or a shadow cutting diagonally across the façade . . . (and if one looks carefully, the same irreducible differences are visible, though the details are of course less distinct, in the rows of windows in *Apartment Houses*). Hopper is painting a world that is not yet dominated by abstract uniformity. For Warhol, abstract uniformity *is* the world.

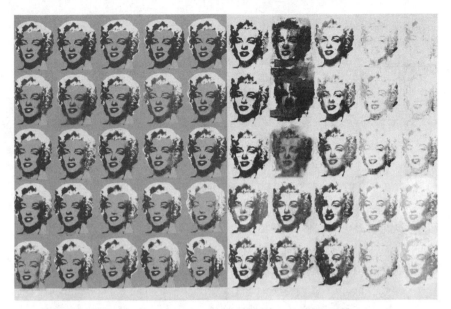

Figure 20.

the Factory, and praised serigraphy—the technique he turned to after the Ferus exhibition closed down—for its "assembly-line effect." Everything seemed ready, in other words, for a full-scale exploration of the universe of American commodities. Then—

August 4, 1962. Then, on the last night of the *Campbell's Soup Cans* exhibition, and not far from there, Marilyn Monroe killed herself. A mere three months later, the *Marilyn Diptych* (Figure 20) was shown in New York. Now at the Tate Modern, the work is composed of fifty images of Marilyn Monroe, arranged in two panels of twenty-five images each: on the left, pink, red, bright orange, yellow, and turquoise; on the right, black and white. A couple of images on the right side are almost entirely hidden by a thick black smear, while the farthest column is so faded, the visages seem to be on the verge of vanishing forever; and it's hard not to interpret the smear as the sign of a sudden catastrophe, and the fading as the gradual disappearance from public memory of a once-famous visage (the brevity of modern fame being of course Warhol's most celebrated quip). *Life and Death of a Film Star*; a bit simple, but powerful. All the more striking, then, that the "death" side of the diptych should be so radically absent from Warhol's future production, where black and white will be forever eclipsed by the bright tints that serigraphy will brazenly, and even vulgarly, superimpose on the underlying visage. Skin, eyes, lips, hair, teeth . . . one feature at a time, Marilyn is literally *covered* by layers of flashy paint—as are Jackie, Mao, Elvis, Liz (they are so famous, Warhol's subjects, that one name is enough). All always changing, because their colors are changing; all changing, and no one *ageing*. The entropic process so central to Rembrandt's conception of the portrait is unimaginable in this world where time doesn't exist, and death can only be the "dagger thrust" of Cinquecento portraits that Simmel had contrasted to Rembrandt's "current," flowing naturally into the ocean of death [74]. For Warhol, as for children, death can only be accidental or deliberate: a car crash; assassination; suicide; electric chair. It's a world where even the old die young.

Pseudo-individuality. Marilyn's face as a human soup can, then? Yes and no. Despite its supposed "assembly-line" quality, Warhol's peculiar use of serigraphy created a mismatch between image and color which generated a whole series of "mechanical deviations" from the given template. One need only compare *Campbell's Soup Cans* with the left panel of the *Marilyn Diptych* (let alone the right one): in order to notice the differences among the thirty-two cans one has to focus on microscopic details; with Marilyn, one immediately notices, here the whiteness of the teeth, there the blue of the eyelids, the curls, the lips, the shadows, the eyebrows . . . Always her, always a little different: thinner, blonder, sadder, sexier, uglier . . . Each replica of the photograph, individualized in its own peculiar way. Or perhaps: *pseudo*-individualized. "In the cultural industry," write Horkheimer and Adorno,

> the individual [is] illusory [. . .] From the standardized improvisation in jazz to the original film personality who must have a lock of hair straying over her eyes so that she can be recognized as such, pseudo-individuality reigns.*

Pseudo-individuality is the result of two converging processes: first, cultural products—be they stories or melodies, styles or images, or indeed celebrities—are relentlessly simplified and standardized; then, individual instances are re-elaborated to make them appear somewhat "unique." Unlike the prosaic world of soups, the cultural market wants its products to be "special," in one way or another; the only trouble is that, by the mid-twentieth century, standardization has become so pervasive that only minutiae like eyelids, lips, or "locks of hair" can still be individualized. Whence the "pseudo" of the *Dialectics*: a way of denouncing this reliance on accessory traits as a parody of the much more demanding—much more *structural*—formation of bourgeois individuality. But that's precisely Warhol's appeal: with him, *nothing* is demanding. One looks at his Marilyn—or his Mao, for that matter—and it really feels like it's all just a matter of makeup.

* Max Horkheimer and Theodor W. Adorno, *Dialectics of Enlightenment*, 1944, Stanford UP, 2002, pp. 124–25.

As long as it's black. But is makeup ever "just" makeup, in the contemporary world? As the "secular stagnation of markets for standardized goods" enveloped the advanced capitalist economies, writes Wolfgang Streeck,

> capital's answer to [. . .] the end of the Fordist era included mak-
> ing goods less standardized, [going] far beyond the yearly
> changes in hubcaps and tail fins that American automakers had
> invented to accelerate product obsolescence [. . .] in an effort to
> get closer to the idiosyncratic preferences of ever-smaller groups
> of potential customers [. . .] By the 1980s, no two cars built on
> the same day at the Volkswagen plant in Wolfsburg were com-
> pletely identical.*

No two identical cars. Who knows whether Warhol had ever heard of Henry Ford's banter about the Model T ("You can have it in any color you want, as long as it's black"); for sure, he spent his life doing exactly the opposite. With him, you can have anybody in any color you want, as long as it's not black. His products are more standardized than cultural forms have ever been—always the same frozen face, the same still from *Niagara*, year after year after year—but the inventiveness of surface variations is such that a pre-fix like "pseudo" no longer sounds right. With an extraordinary historical intuition, Warhol's work combined "Fordist" *and* "post-Fordist" models, using the latter to revamp the former: always the same photo, as if his paintings were so many 1920s Model Ts—but with the endlessly varied extras of 1980s Wolfsburg. Given that ac-cessories cannot have a life of their own, independent of the

---

*Wolfgang Streeck, *How Will Capitalism End?*, Verso, London and New York, 2016, pp. 98–99.

structures of which they are part, one could say that the products of the Factory have never really transcended the horizon of the cultural Fordism described in *Dialectics of Enlightenment*. Which is true, but misses the point of Warhol's contribution to American cultural hegemony: accepting without reservations the existing state of affairs (always the same photo of the same face), but making it as interesting and pleasant as possible (always a new alteration of one kind or another). Just like the "personalized" extras of the post-Fordist era, the colorful variations of a Warhol portrait series embody a symbolic "pact" in which the aesthetics of the detail plays a disproportionate role in the perception of contemporary commodities. It is the thorough understanding—and exploitation—of this logic that has placed Andy Warhol at the aesthetic center of the Age of the Accessory in which we are all still living.

Illustration Credits

p. 67: *Stagecoach*, 1939. United Artists / Photofest.

p. 67: Barbara Stanwyck and Fred McMurray in *Double Indemnity*. Paramount Pictures / Photofest.

p. 77: *Masterson of Kansas* / Everett Collection.

p. 80: *Double Indemnity*. Paramount Pictures / Photofest.

p. 81: *The Third Man*. Selznick Releasing / Photofest.

p. 83: *The Lady from Shanghai*. Columbia Pictures / Photofest.

p. 89: *The Third Man*. Selznick Releasing / Photofest.

p. 108: *Girl Interrupted at Her Music* by Jan (Johannes) Vermeer (1632–75), c. 1658–69 (oil on canvas), © The Frick Collection.

p. 110: *Sunday* by Edward Hopper, 1926 (oil on canvas) / The Phillips Collection, Washington, D.C., USA / Acquired 1926 / Bridgeman Images, © Heirs of Josephine Hopper / Licensed by VAGA, New York, NY.

p. 111: *Automat* by Edward Hopper, 1927, oil on canvas, Des Moines Art Center, Des Moines, Iowa, USA / De Agostini Picture Library / Bridgeman Images, © Heirs of Josephine Hopper / Licensed by VAGA, New York, NY.

p. 113: *Room in New York* by Edward Hopper, 1932 (oil on canvas) / Sheldon Museum of Art, University of Nebraska, Lincoln, USA / Bridgeman Images, © Heirs of Josephine Hopper / Licensed by VAGA, New York, NY.

p. 113: *The Love Letter* by Johannes Vermeer, c. 1669–70 (oil on canvas) / Courtesy of the Rijksmuseum.

p. 115: *Drug Store* by Edward Hopper, 1927 (oil on canvas) / Museum of Fine Arts, Boston, Massachusetts, USA / Bequest of John T. Spaulding / Bridgeman Images, © Heirs of Josephine Hopper / Licensed by VAGA, New York, NY.

p. 119: *Self-Portrait* by Harmensz van Rijn Rembrandt, c. 1629 (oil on wood) / Indianapolis Museum of Art at Newfields, USA / The Clowes Fund Collection / Bridgeman Images.

p. 120: *Self-Portrait* by Harmensz van Rijn Rembrandt, c. 1657. Artist/Creator: Harmensz van Rijn Rembrandt Kunsthistorisches Museum, Vienna, Austria, Netherlands, 1657, © Imagno / Austrian Archives / The Image Works.

p. 121: *Self-Portrait* by Harmensz van Rijn Rembrandt, 1659 (oil on canvas) / Andrew W. Mellon Collection, National Gallery of Art, Washington, D.C., USA.

p. 123: *Campbell's Soup Cans* by Andy Warhol, 1962, © 2018 The Andy Warhol Foundation for the Visual Arts, Inc. / Licensed by Artists Rights Society (ARS), New York. Photograph © The Museum of Modern Art / Licensed by SCALA / Art Resource, NY.

p. 125: *Warhol Diptych* by Andy Warhol, 1973 (silkscreen inks, synthetic polymer, and acrylic on canvas), Elaine Sturtevant (1924–2014) / Private Collection. Photo © Christie's Images / Bridgeman Images, © 2018 The Andy Warhol Foundation for the Visual Arts, Inc. / Licensed by Artists Rights Society (ARS), New York. Marilyn Monroe™; Rights of Publicity and Persona Rights: The Estate of Marilyn Monroe LLC. 2018, marilynmonroe.com.